Leading The Cooperative School

David W. Johnson

Roger T. Johnson

Interaction Book Company

7208 Cornelia Drive

Edina, Minnesota 55435

(612) 831-9500

Johnson & Johnson

This book is dedicated to the hundreds of individuals who
have taken our training in how to lead their districts in
implementing cooperative learning to create classroom
environments where students care about each other and
each other's learning.

ISBN 0-939603-08-X

Table of Contents

Preface   I : 04

Chapter 1: Creating The Cooperative School   1 : 01

Chapter 2: Leading A Loosely Coupled Organization   2 : 01

Chapter 3: Research On Cooperative Learning   3 : 01

Chapter 4: Cooperative Learning   4 : 01

Chapter 5: Promoting Teachers' Instructional Expertise   5 : 01

Chapter 6: Structuring Colleagial Support Groups   6 : 01

Chapter 7: Structuring School Task Forces   7 : 01

Chapter 8: Structuring Ad Hoc Decision-Making Groups   8 : 01

Chapter 9: Leading By Example / Encouraging The Heart   9 : 01

Chapter 10: The Stars And The Ground   10 : 01

Preface

This book is about how school leaders can get extraordinary things done in the school. It is about how you, the reader, can turn challenging opportunities into remarkable successes. There are no shortages of challenging opportunities within schools. Getting extraordinary things done, furthermore, is not restricted to a select few stars or a select few schools. It is something the vast majority of school staff members are capable of doing.

This book is about leading people, not merely managing them. **Leadership begins where management ends, where the systems of rewards and punishments, control and scrutiny, give way to innovation, individual character, and the courage of convictions.** Your challenge is to lead your staff to get extraordinary things done. This requires inspiring and motivating your staff toward a common purpose and building a cohesive and spirited team. Your staff has to be friends with you and each other.

Having a staff that cares about each other, both personally and professionally, is difficult in a "loosely coupled" organization. Individuals cannot care for someone they never interact or work with. Organizing the staff so that they do in fact interact with each other is a prerequisite for creating a cohesive team striving to achieve mutual goals.

How staff members interact with each other as they instruct students and run the school has been relatively ignored, despite its powerful effects. Staff relationships may be structured so that teachers compete to see who is best, ignore each other and work independently, or work together cooperatively. The extensive research comparing these interaction patterns clearly suggests that cooperation among staff members produces greater productivity, greater motivation, more positive relationships among staff members, greater acceptance of differences, higher professional self-esteem, and a number of other outcomes than do competition or working individualistically. At the same time, leaders have been taught and encouraged to prevent staff members from helping each other, talking to each other, or encouraging each other.

This book is about demonstrating leadership by structuring work situations cooperatively, so that staff members work together to achieve shared goals. Cooperation is an old idea. Shifting the emphasis from working alone to working together and caring about whether colleagues are working productively is a relatively simple idea. Implementing it is not. This book contains a set of practical strategies for structuring cooperative teams. Gaining a high level of expertise in implementing cooperative strategies is not easy. It will take some training, perseverence, and support. The training that has been planned to go with these chapters should provide a good start, but it may take a year or two of experience before structuring cooperative efforts becomes integrated and natural. Persisting until you can use cooperative procedures and strategies at a routine-use level will benefit your staff members and students in numerous ways. It is well worth your efforts.

It has taken us nearly 25 years to build the theory, research, and practical experience required to write this book. In the 1960's we began by reviewing the research, conducting our initial research studies, and training teachers in the classroom use of cooperation (Johnson, 1970). Since then our work has proliferated. Our more recent writings on cooperative learning include **Cooperation In The Classroom** (Johnson, Johnson, & Holubec, 1984, 1988), **Learning Together and Alone** (Johnson & Johnson, 1975, 1987) and **Circles of Learning** (Johnson, Johnson, & Holubec, 1986). Related work on interpersonal skills may be found in our books such as **Reaching Out** (Johnson, 1986), and **Joining Together** (Johnson & F. Johnson, 1987). Recently we have published **Creative Conflict** (Johnson & Johnson, 1987a), a book on the classroom use of conflict to teach students how to manage conflicts within cooperative learning groups constructively. Yet the concept of cooperative learning is much, much older than our work. Our roots reach back to Morton Deutsch and then to Kurt Lewin. We wish to acknowledge our indebtedness to the work of both of these social psychologists.

Our debt to Judy Bartlett is unmeasurable. Her talents, her dedication, and her work beyond the call of duty have all contributed to the completion of this book. We are continually impressed with and are grateful for her work. She also believes in cooperative learning and often works beyond the call of duty to ensure that it is shared with students in the classroom.

Chapter 1

Creating The Cooperative School

The Cooperative School

On July 15, 1982, Don Bennett, a Seattle businessman, was the first amputee ever to climb Mount Rainier (reported in Kouzes & Posner, 1987). He climbed 14,410 feet on one leg and two crutches. It took him five days. When asked to state the most important lesson he learned from doing so, without hesitation he said, "You can't do it alone."

Schools are not buildings, curriculums, and machines. **Schools are relationships and interactions among people.** It is the interaction patterns among students, between students and teachers, among teachers, between teachers and administrators, and among administrators that determine how effective schools are. There are three ways that interactions within the school may be structured: competitively (so individuals compete to see who is best), individualistically (so everyone works on his or her own, independent from each other), and cooperatively (so individuals work together to achieve mutual goals). Which one of these interaction patterns dominates school life has profound and widespread impact on school effectiveness.

You can walk into any school or classroom and immediately decrease achievement and productivity. It's easy. All it takes is two messages to students and/or staff members:

1. You are isolated and alone.

2. This is a serious competition to see who is the winner and who are the losers.

As anxiety and apprehension go up, performance goes down. As individuals believe they have no chance to win, motivation ceases. As self-concepts become negative, people stop trying. As the shame of being a loser is driven home, absences due to physical illness and psychological misery occur more frequently.

The extensive research comparing the relative efficacy of cooperative, competitive, and individualistic efforts clearly indicates that cooperation among staff members produces greater productivity, achievement, and motivation; more positive, caring, and committed relationships; greater acceptance and appreciation of differences; greater social support and assistance; higher self-esteem and psychological well-being; and greater mastery of important social skills such as leadership, trust, communication, and conflict skills (see Chapter 3). The amount of research, and the consistency of the findings provide ample verification of the power of working together to get the job done. Even seemingly individual extraordinary efforts have their roots in cooperative relationships. Don Bennett is an example.

During one very difficult trek across an ice field in Don Bennett's hop to the top of Mount Rainer, his daughter stayed by his side for four hours and with each new hop told him, "You can do it, Dad. You're the best dad in the world. You can do it, Dad." There was no way Bennett would quit hopping to the top with his daughter yelling words of love and encouragement in his ear. The encouragement by his daughter kept him going, strengthening his commitment to make it to the top. The classroom and school are similar. With members of their cooperative group cheering them on, students amaze themselves and their teachers with what they can achieve. With members of their colleagial support group cheering them on, teachers amaze themselves and their colleagues with what they can accomplish with their use of cooperative learning.

While decreasing student achievement and staff productivity is easy, increasing them is not. It is much harder to establish cooperation than it is to destroy it. To be effective, the school has to be a cooperative place. Your effectiveness as a principal depends on how successfully you can establish cooperative relationships among staff members, among students, and between staff members and students. The **cooperative school** consists of:

1. **Cooperative learning in the classroom:** This means using three types of cooperative learning groups:

   a. **Formal cooperative learning groups** that complete specific tasks and assignments such as solving math problems, completing instructional units, writing reports or themes, conducting experiments, and reading stories, plays, or books.

   b. **Informal cooperative learning groups** that are temporary, ad hoc groups used as part of lecturing and direct teaching to focus student attention on the material to be learned, create an expectation set and mood conducive to learning, ensure students cognitively process the material being taught, and provide closure to an instructional session.

   c. **Cooperative base groups** that are long-term groups (lasting for one semester or year) with stable membership whose primary responsibility is to give each member the support, encouragement, and assistance he or she needs to make academic progress.

2. **Cooperative staff-teams in the school:** This means using three types of staff teams:

a. **Colleagial support groups** to increase teachers' instructional expertise and success.

b. **Task forces** that plan and implement solutions to school-wide issues and problems such as curriculum adoptions and lunchroom behavior.

c. **Ad hoc decision-making groups** that are used during faculty meetings to involve all staff members in important school decisions.

To qualify as a cooperative school, cooperation must dominate both student and faculty life. This requires quite a transformation. Classrooms are dominated by competitive-individualistic learning. Staffs are dominated by competitive-individualistic interaction. Teachers cannot be ordered to teach cooperatively. Teachers can only be inspired to do so. Teachers must become committed to implementing cooperative learning within their classrooms and to engaging in cooperative efforts with their colleagues. **Inspiring teachers to become committed to creating a cooperative school takes leadership.** Leadership begins where management ends, where rewards and punishments used to control behavior give way to a common purpose, innovation, teamwork, and the courage of convictions.

Being A Leader, Not A Manager

There is growth and decline. Staying the same is not an option. Growth takes leadership, not management. There is a difference. Some individuals manage, some individuals lead. The difference may be found in the root meanings of "lead" and "manage" (Kouzes & Posner, 1987). The root origin of **lead** is a word meaning "to go," denoting travel from one place to another. Leaders are those who "go first," pioneering unexplored territory and showing others the direction they should take. By comparison, the root origin of **manage** is a word meaning "hand." Managing seems to connote "handling" things by controlling and maintaining the status quo. Managers tend to handle things, leaders tend to get us going somewhere. **The unique role of the leader is to take us on journeys to places we have never been before.**

The metaphor of the journey may be the most appropriate metaphor for discussing the tasks of leaders. Individuals can manage what now exists, the status quo, or take staff members on a journey to increase their expertise and create a new and better school.

Perhaps more than anything else, leadership is about the creation of a new way of life within schools. Leadership is inextricably connected with the process of innovation, of bringing new ideas, methods, or solutions into use. Leaders are agents of change. Change requires leadership, a "prime mover" to push for implementation of strategic decisions. The leader highlights the challenges the school faces and makes them shared challenges for the staff. **Leaders create a "family" within which staff members care deeply about each other and the mutual vision they are trying to actualize.** Managers get other people to do, but leaders get other people to **want** to do. Managers get staff members to teach students. Leaders get staff members to **want** to teach students.

Providing Leadership To Inspire Teachers' Courage

"People cannot be managed. Inventories can be managed, but people must be led."

H. Ross Perot, Founder, Electronic Data Systems

In order to discuss how best to provide leadership to a school, it may be helpful to compare two schools, one in which staff members work in isolation from each other and generally compete to see who is the best teacher, and one in which staff members interact frequently within cooperative work groups. In the **first school,** teachers essentially teach in isolation from one another and associate with each other only at lunch, except for small friendship cliques. Members of different cliques tend to find fault with each other, blame and ridicule each other, show disrespect for and distrust each other, and challenge each other's statements and ideas. Teachers speak of "us vs. them" in antagonistic ways. Teacher energy is focused on the incompetence of colleagues and the administration, the latest "dumb thing" certain teachers and administrators did this week, how to beat the evaluation process, and what is the latest grievance.

In the **cooperative school**, teachers spend some time each day working with colleagues to (1) support each other's efforts to improve their expertise as teachers and (2) solve current problems faced by the school. Teachers walk through each other's classrooms. At lunch, they share ideas about more effective teaching and classroom management. Teachers working on grade-level teams share materials and tips. A pupil-assistance-team leads an inservice to discuss better ways to mainstream students. Teacher energy is spent planning for their teaching, helping and assisting each other, and working on schoolwide tasks. Teachers talk about social events for the faculty and the administration, speak highly of the principal's skills, and seek out the principal's assistance on solving teaching problems.

Effective schools are those that produce students (equally across ethnic membership, national origin, cr social class) who have mastered the required knowledge and skills to move to higher education, to work successfully in a career or vocation, and generally to be productive citizens in our society and world. As schools exist to educate students, the most important responsibility of the principal is to promote the instructional expertise of teachers. **The leader's worst nightmare** is a teacher who is stuck in the status quo, teaching the same way today he or she taught 10 years ago, and planning to continue the present methods of instruction until formal retirement. Such teachers are often known as being "retired in place." **The leader's dream** is a teacher who has a vision of significantly influencing students' learning and development and has the courage to modify and improve instructional practices continually in order to be more and more successful. The latter type teachers are not born. They are created through effective leadership.

Whether staff members choose to stick with the status quo or attempt to grow professionally is a **personal choice involving risk, anxiety, and courage**. Whether staff members choose to increase their professional expertise or cling to the past depends in large part on the encouragement, support, and acceptance they receive from the principal and peers. The lower the support and acceptance a staff member feels, the more likely he or she will be to cling inappropriately to past procedures and strategies. It takes a colleagial support system to provide these teachers with the security and support they need to risk changing their instructional practices.

This book is about leading to inspire, promote, support, and encourage individual acts of courage by teachers to leave the security of the status quo and to grow professionally. The success of the school depends on the instructional expertise of the teachers. Expertise is **not** something that is gained and then enjoyed forever. It is a process. **Either teachers are seeking to increase their instructional expertise or else they are losing it.** A teacher is either growing or dying professionally. And to grow they must have a dream of what their teaching could be. They must have the courage to stand up and say, "The way I am presently teaching is not the way I always want to teach. Alternatives exist. I could be better. I will be better."

For teachers to admit that their teaching could be better requires courage. It requires courage because in many schools taking risks to increase one's competence is not rewarded. One of the paradoxes of schools is that there is unceasing conflict between what school success requires and what the realities of school life reward. School success requires that teachers continually strive to improve their instructional expertise. School reality is that the teachers who are rewarded are those who state that they have arrived, that they are instructional experts, that they have everything under control, that there is no student they cannot handle, that they understand their subject matter areas thoroughly, and that they are outstanding at what they do. To seek to grow and develop is to admit current shortcomings and dissatisfaction with the status quo. This takes courage. **The primary responsibility of the principal is to foster a school climate in which teachers have the courage to challenge their current instructional practices and strive to grow and develop professionally.**

It is not that teachers and other staff members lack courage. Most staff members at some time act courageously through bold action and quiet modification of current practices. But the acts of cowardice and conformity are all too frequent and teachers continue the status quo of lecture, whole-class discussion, individual worksheets, and competitive tests. **Leadership strategies and procedures are needed that stimulate, not stifle, acts of courage by teachers.**

Leading Teachers For Instructional Excellence

> *"Leadership appears to be the art of getting others to want to do something that you are convinced should be done."*

> Vance Packard, **The Pyramid Climbers**

In order to be a leader, others must choose to follow you. Followers determine whether someone is a leader. A superintendent cannot confer leadership when he or she appoints people to the position of principal. Leadership is in the eye of the follower. Recently Kouzes and Posner (1987) reported on a series of studies on how leaders are perceived by their followers. Before most people are willing to perceive someone as a leader, they must believe that he or she is honest, competent, forward-looking, and inspiring. These qualities make a manager a credible leader. Staff members want to assure themselves that the principal is an honest person who has integrity, is worthy of their trust, and behaves consistently with what he or she says. Staff members want to know that the principal has the skills, attitudes, competencies, and courage to lead. Staff members want to know that the principal has a sense of direction and a clear view of what the school will be like in the future. Finally, staff members want to be inspired by the commitment, enthusiasm, energy, and positiveness of the principal.

It is not easy to influence teachers to experiment with new instructional practices, as many teachers will resist due to their liking for the status quo, resting on past laurels, and lacking commitment to teaching excellence. Many teachers believe that nothing is wrong with their current instructional practices. They tend to tolerate only modest innovations that do not require major changes in instructional practices. Other teachers will rest on their past laurels. In many school districts that have reputations for being excellent, teachers have stopped striving to improve their instructional expertise, pointing to their past success as the reason for their complacency. Finally, many teachers have lost what made them so successful in the first place: commitment to professional growth and a willingness to take risks in experimenting with new instructional strategies and practices. They no longer have the will to take risks to get things done better, sooner, faster, and more effectively. They feel safe in the status quo.

One of the leader's responsibilities is to create a school structure that inspires teachers to recognize the limitations of their current instructional practices and strive to improve their instructional expertise.

The Principal And School Productivity

"The hottest places in Hell are reserved for those who, in a time of great moral crisis, maintain their neutrality."

Dante

There are a series of leadership issues principals have to face in order to maximize the productivity of the school (Kouzes & Posner, 1987):

1. How to **challenge the status quo** of the traditional competitive and individualistic models of teaching.

2. How to **inspire a clear mutual vision** of what the school should and could be, a clear mission that all staff members are committed to achieving, and a set of goals that guide staff members' efforts.

3. How to **empower staff members through cooperative team work** within colleagial support groups, task forces, and ad hoc decision-making groups. Doing so enables each individual staff member to take action to increase his or her expertise and effectiveness.

4. How to **lead by example** by (a) using cooperative procedures and (b) taking risks to increase professional expertise.

5. How to **encourage the heart** of staff members to persist and keep striving to improve their expertise in using cooperative learning and teaching.

Challenging The Competitive / Individualistic Status Quo

The status quo is the competitive / individualistic structure that dominates schools and classrooms. In the classroom, it is represented by: (a) listening to lectures, (b) participating in whole-class discussions, (c) completing individual worksheets, and (d) taking the test on Friday. In most classrooms this represents 80 - 90 percent of the students' day. In the school, the competitive / individualistic structure is represented by individual teachers working in their own classroom, instructing their own students, at their own pace, striving toward their own goals and priorities, while being worried about where they rank in teaching effectiveness in their school. Leaders challenge the effectiveness of these current instructional and organizational practices.

Leaders are pioneers who are willing to take risks to innovate and experiment to find new and better ways of instructing students. This does not mean that leaders are the creators or originators of new instructional methods and better teaching. **The leader's primary contribution is in recognizing good ideas, supporting those ideas, and being willing to challenge the status quo in order to get new teaching practices implemented.** In essence, leaders are early adopters of innovations.

There is a history of individual initiative in America. America has been a country in which old traditions are challenged and, if they are found wanting, discarded. American folklore is filled with examples of guts, know-how, and instances where an individual seeking to solve a problem moved aside social convention and traditional authority in order to do so. As Henry Steele Commager writes:

> *"Every pioneer who pulled up stakes and headed for the frontier registered...a vote of dissent from the past...The American way was always taking a short-cut to freedom, a short-cut to fortune, a short-cut to learning, and a short-cut to heaven."*

Leaders inspire staff members to recognize that **if they are not working to increase their expertise, they are losing their expertise.** Expertise is a process, not an end product. Any person or organization is constantly changing. If expertise is not growing, then it is declining. The minute a person believes he or she is an expert and stops trying to learn more, then he or she is losing their expertise. **Leaders must lead staff members toward enhanced expertise, not manage for bureaucratic control. And the clearest and**

most direct challenge to traditional competitive and individualistic teaching is the adoption of cooperative learning.

Our Dream: Establishing A Joint Vision, Mission, And Goals

The second leadership responsibility is to create a joint vision of what the school should and could be, a clear mission that all staff members are committed to achieving, and a set of goals that guide staff members' efforts. **To do so an individual must:**

1. Have a vision/dream of what the school could be.

2. Communicate that vision with commitment and enthusiasm.

3. Make it a **shared** vision that staff members adopt as their own.

4. Make it a rational vision based on theory and research and sound implementation procedures.

Leaders enthusiastically and frequently communicate the dream of classrooms and the school being places where individuals share, help, encourage, and support each other's efforts to achieve and succeed. Places where **we** dominates **me.** Where working together to get the job done creates caring and committed relation- ships that propel people forward in their mutual search for excel- lence.

Every excellent school begins with a dream. Leaders often see the results of improved instructional practices more clearly than do nonleaders. It is their image of the future that pulls the staff for- ward. The vision clarifies the mission and goals of the school and reminds staff members of the adage, "Before working on being efficient by doing the job right, be effective by doing the right job!"

There is an old Texas saying, **"You can't light a fire with a wet match."** Leaders cannot ignite the flame of passion in staff members if the leaders themselves do not express enthusiasm for a compelling vision. The vision that binds committed school staff members together needs to be communicated to the staff clearly, explicitly, insistently, proactively, and persistently, over and over again. Steve Jobs, one of the founders of Apple Corporation, when asked what the primary responsibility of an executive is, stated, "Keeper of the dream." **The administrator or staff member, as a leader, is the keeper of the dream within the school.** When promoting cooperative learning, for example, the leader has to believe in it and advocate it without hesitation. The leader's convictions should show.

Leaders inspire a **shared** vision. It is the common vision that creates a basic sense of "sink or swim together" (i.e., positive interdependence) among staff members and students. Leaders breathe life into the hopes and dreams of others and enable them to see the exciting possibilities the future holds by striving for a common purpose. A person with no followers is **not** a leader, and people will not become followers until they accept a vision as their own. It is the long-term promise of achieving something worthwhile and meaningful that powers an individual's drive toward greater expertise. A principal cannot order teachers to use cooperative learning. He or she has to persuade or inspire teachers to do so. It is teacher commitment that determines how frequently cooperative learning is used, not memo's from the principal. **You cannot command commitment, you can only inspire it!**

Finally, **the vision and its advocacy has to be rational**. The new instructional practices have to be backed up with a knowledge of the relevant research and theory. And the procedures for implementing new instructional strategies within the school have to be logical and sound.

Empowering Staff Through Cooperative Teams

A student says, "I can't do algebra! It's too hard. I'll never understand it!" What does a teacher do to combat students' feelings of helplessness? The answer to this question is, "Give them learning partners and have them work cooperatively." A teacher says, "I can't replan my lessons to be cooperative. I don't have time. I have two children of my own, they have to be driven to lessons every night, my spouse expects me to do half the housework which takes up all my weekends. I just do not have the time and energy to prepare better lessons!" What does a leader do to combat teachers' feelings of helplessness? The answer to that question is, "Give them colleagues and have them work cooperatively in upgrading their instructional skills."

The most important of all the five leadership practices is empowering individuals by organizing them into cooperative teams. To be effective a cooperative team must be carefully structured to include positive interdependence, face-to-face promotive interaction, individual accountability, social skills, and group processing (Johnson, Johnson, & Holubec, 1986, 1988). In the classroom the teacher uses three types of cooperative learning groups:

1. **Formal cooperative learning groups** complete a specific task or assignment such as solving a set of math problems, completing an instructional unit, writing a report or theme, conducting an experiment, and reading a story, play, chapter, or book.

2. **Informal cooperative learning groups** are temporary, ad hoc groups used as part of lecturing and direct teaching to focus student attention on the material to be learned, create an expectation set and mood conducive to learning, ensure

students cognitively process the material being taught, and provide closure to an instructional session.

3. **Cooperative base groups** are long-term groups (lasting for at least one semester or year) with stable membership whose primary responsibility is to give each member the support, encouragement, and assistance he or she needs to make educational progress.

The cooperative school begins in the classroom. The use of cooperative learning is the first step in working cooperatively with colleagues. Cooperative learning is discussed in Chapters 3 and 4.

What is good for students, is even better for faculty. To lead the school effectively, the leader needs to employ three types of cooperative groups:

1. **Colleagial support groups** to increase teachers' instructional expertise and success.

2. **Task force groups** to plan and implement solutions to schoolwide issues and problems such as curriculum adoptions and lunchroom behavior.

3. **Ad hoc decision-making groups** used during faculty meetings to involve all staff members in important school decisions.

The one-word test to detect whether someone is on the road to becoming a leader is **we**. Leaders do not achieve success by themselves. It is not **my** personal best leaders inspire, it is **our** personal best. The most important thing a leader can do is to organize staff members so that they work cooperatively with each other, for at least two reasons.

The first is to promote committed and caring relationships among staff members. This is achieved through a "team" approach. Having teachers work as part of cooperative teams fosters committed and caring relationships. Cooperative efforts result in trust, open communication, and interpersonal support and caring among staff, all of which are crucial ingredients to teacher productivity and school success. When trust is broken by competition, harsh feelings, criticism, negative comments, and disrespect, productivity suffers.

The second is to empower staff members through teamwork. By organizing staff members into cooperative teams, leaders increase staff members' confidence that if they exert effort, they will be successful. Teams empower their members to act by making them feel strong, capable, and committed. Being part of a team enables teachers to innovate, experiment, take risks, and grow professionally.

There are many advantages of cooperative over competitive and individualistic efforts by staff members (Johnson & Johnson, 1983, in press; Johnson, Johnson, & Holubec, 1986). The amount of research validating the power of well-structured cooperative efforts is staggering. Working cooperatively to get the job done results in greater productivity and achievement, more frequent higher-level conceptual reasoning and critical thinking, more frequent oral explanation and elaboration, more peer encouragement and support for task efforts, more positive attitudes toward work and learning, higher self-esteem, and greater social skills. These findings are supported by observation studies that have found that participation in cooperative, colleagial groups can expand teachers' levels of expertise by supplying a source of intellectual provocation and new ideas (e.g., Little, 1981; Shulman & Carey, 1984). Collaboration among teachers breaks the grip of psychological isolation from other adults that characterizes the teacher's workplace (Sarason, 1971) and creates a forum for teachers to publicly test their ideas about teaching (Lortie, 1975). The "real world" involves working with and through many different people to get the job done. Schools should not be different.

Once staff members are organized into cooperative groups, the next issue is providing them with the necessary training in interpersonal and small group skills. It takes considerable skill to be a productive member of a cooperative group. Of special importance are the skills in managing conflicts constructively.

Colleagial Support Groups

The leader structures colleagial support groups aimed at building and maintaining teachers' instructional expertise. Colleagial support groups will be discussed at length in Chapter 5. Their purpose is to improve members' professional competence and ensure members' professional growth. In organizing colleagial support groups the leader needs to keep in mind that membership is voluntary and inclusive. The leader approaches teachers he or she believes are interested, invites them to participate, networks them together, provides them with resources, and reinforces their efforts. Membership is inclusive, not exclusive. New members are always welcome.

In forming colleagial support groups the leader must recognize that **it is personal commitment, not authority, that energizes change efforts by teachers.** Participation in the colleagial support groups is aimed at increasing teachers' belief that they are engaged in a joint venture ("We are doing it!"), public commitment to peers to increase their instructional expertise ("I will try it!"), peer accountability ("They are counting on me!"), sense of social support ("They will help and assist me!"), sense of safety ("The risk is challenging but not excessive!"), and self-efficacy ("If I exert the effort, I will be successful!").

School Task Groups

Sam Jones was running through the announcements at a faculty meeting. *"There is increasing concern about the amount of littering taking place in the lunchroom, hallways, and school grounds. The problem has increased dramatically this year. I have asked Jane, Jim, Joan, and Jeremy to serve as a task force to consider the problem and make a recommendation to the faculty as to how it may be solved. Please give them any assistance they ask for. As soon as they have a recommendation ready, we will discuss the issue in a faculty meeting and decide what to do."*

There are school issues that call for assessment and planning. Curriculum adoptions, inservice education, bus schedules, playground supervision, decreasing drug use by students, ensuring appropriate behavior in hallways and lunchrooms, school-parent communications, and many other issues that require considered planning and action by the school staff. The leader organizes a faculty task group, gives it its charge and a schedule, and then provides the resources required for the group to function. The group then brings a recommendation to the faculty. Membership is not strictly voluntary as teachers are asked to serve.

Task groups are small problem-solving groups that diagnose a problem, gather data about the causes and extent of the problem, consider a variety of alternative solutions, make conclusions, and present a recommendation to the faculty as a whole. Thus, teachers need to be trained in identifying problems, analyzing problems, hypothesizing major causes, verifying the existence of problems, identifying potential solutions, deciding on a recommendation, and presenting that recommendation persuasively to the whole staff.

Ad Hoc Decision-Making Groups

Mary Field stood up and faced her staff. "We have just heard the recommendation of the task force on littering in the lunchroom, hallways, and school grounds. There are 27 staff members in attendence. I am going to count off by 9 to make groups of three. Each triad is to decide whether to accept or reject the recommendation of the task force and state their rationale for doing so. You are to come to consensus within the triad. Everyone should agree with the decision and be able to explain the rationale. I will randomly pick one teacher from each triad to explain their triad's rationale and decision. We will then discuss the recommendation briefly and take a vote of the entire faculty to decide whether or not to accept the task force's recommendation."

During faculty meetings the school staff will be asked to make decisions about school policy and what recommendations should be adopted to solve schoolwide problems. The most effective way of making such decisions is to implement a small-group / large group procedure involving **ad hoc decision-making groups in which staff members listen to the recommendation, are assigned to small groups (usually three members), meet in the small groups and consider the recommendation, decide whether to accept or reject the recommendation and why, report to the entire faculty their decision and rationale, and then discuss and decide in the staff as a whole.** Such a procedure maximizes the participation and involvement of all staff members in the school's decision making.

Leading Through Teams

Almost every executive in almost every organization states that teamwork, people cooperating to achieve goals, is essential in their organization and their own work unit. They recognize that **work output is a function of group identity and the feelings of social support and cohesion that come with increased interaction among team members.** This is as true for schools as it is for business and industry. But very few school districts institute a district-wide program to ensure team effectiveness, and relatively few leaders institute a systematic team-building process on their own without district support. Few school districts carry out a systematic program for developing organization teams. **Administrators seem to believe that their staffs ought to know how to work together without any formal training or development activity and that they will do so, on their own, without any encouragement or mandate to do so.**

Nothing could be farther from the truth. Most staff members do not know how to function as part of a team and rarely do so. Common statements about experiences in working as part of teams include:

"It is no fun working with those people. They seem uncommitted to their own teaching and they do not want to help anyone else teach better."

"Our meetings are chaos. Nobody listens. Nobody supports anyone else. We just argue unproductively or sit silently waiting for the meeting to be over."

"We never do anything teamlike. We do not set goals, we do not plan, we do not teach together. Everyone goes back to his or her classroom and teaches in isolation from everyone else."

"I do not trust anyone that I work with. They would all knife you in the back if they thought it would help their cause. At times they can act friendly, but when the crunch comes, it is each person for himself."

"People talk about teamwork around here, but I do not know what that means. I go to work, sit at my desk, and teach my classes. From time to time I go to meetings, which are usually a waste of time. I get a yearly performance review, which has not changed much in years, and I draw my pay. I do not see what teamwork means in my job."

"My principal is so busy that he does not even talk about how our staff could be organized into effective teams. He has his favorites whom he talks to, but the rest of us just do our work and hardly ever have any significant involvement with him."

Many teachers claim they have **never** been part of a satisfying work team in the school. It is difficult for such teachers to engage in and sustain a team-building program since they really do not know what they are trying to achieve. They do not know what actions are needed to ensure team success. They do not know what an effective team is.

To be effective team members teachers must first **conceptually understand** the three types of teams used within the school, how they are supposed to function, and what is required of members. They then have to **commit** themselves to being good team members. There is no substitute for staff members making a mutual commitment to try to work together effectively. Then they have to **practice. Teams** are collections of staff members who must rely on group collaboration if each member is to experience the optimum success and goal achievement. Good teamwork requires practicing how to function as a team. Considerable practice is needed if the team is going to operate effectively. As part of that practice, teams have to **process** how well they are functioning and what they need to do to improve their coordination and cooperation. While some leaders organize staff members into teams, they rarely encourage the practicing and processing necessary for team success.

Most staff members are only vaguely aware that modern society is a complex of interdependent groups or teams. People are required to work together in the family, in clubs, in churches, in community and service organizations, and on their jobs. One of your responsibilities as a principal is to organize your staff into teams and help the teams function effectively. **All teams need good leadership.**

Teams may be organized in at least four ways--like a golf team, like a baseball team, like a football team, and like a basketball team. Members of a **golf team** all function independently of each other, working to promote as high an individual score as possible, so that when individual scores are combined into team scores their team wins. Members of a **baseball team** are relatively independent of one another and, while all members are required to be on the field together, they virtually never interact together all at the same time. Members of a **football team** are divided into three subteams--offense, defense, and special team. When the subteam is on the field, every player is involved in every play. But the teamwork required is centered in the subteam, not the total team. A **basketball team** is small and all players play on only one team. Every player is involved in all aspects of the game, offense and defense, and all must pass, run, and shoot. When a substitute comes in, all must play with the new person. True teamwork is like a basketball situation where division of effort is meshed into a single coordinated result; where the whole is more, and different, than the sum of its individual parts.

Leaders are like coaches. **Leaders must be able to look at the team effort with a practiced eye, see what is interfering with maximum effort or find out what the blocks are, and then devise a strategy or plan to remove the obstacles and release people for maximum effort as they combine their resources to achieve common goals.** Most leaders, however, are stopped from solving team problems either because they do not see what the real problems are or because they do not know exactly what to do. This book is intended to help leaders overcome both these obstacles, by providing a sound basis for making a correct diagnosis and by outlining team-building procedures that have proved to be effective.

Leading By Example

One does not improve through argument but through examples...Be what you wish to make others become. Make yourself, not your words, a sermon.

Henri Frederic Amiel

To provide school leadership, you will need to model (a) using cooperative procedures and (b) taking risks to increase professional expertise. You model the way by practicing what you are preaching. **You lead by example.** To do so, you must be clear about your belief in cooperative efforts, you must be able to speak coherently about your vision and values, and your actions must be congruent with your words. **You begin leadership by becoming a role model that exemplifies the organizational and leadership values you believe are important.** If you want teachers to use cooperative learning in the classroom, you must use cooperative procedures in faculty meetings. You show your priorities through living your values.

One thing you can count on for certain. **Every exceptional leader is a learner.** The self-confidence required to lead comes from trying, failing, learning from mistakes, and trying again. We are all involved in a continuous process of increasing our professional expertise. From making your own journey to actualize your vision, you model the way for your staff members.

Encouraging The Heart Of Staff Members

"Love 'em and lead 'em."

Major General John H. Stanford, Commander, U.S. Army

Leaders are vigilant about the little things that make a big difference. Each spring at Verstec, annual bonuses are given to about 2,000 nonmanagerial personnel (Kouzes and Posner, 1987). In a recent year, the president arrived at the celebration dressed in a satin costume, riding atop an elephant, and accompanied by the Stanford Marching Band. The president frequently says, "If you are going to give someone a check, don't just mail it. Have a celebration."

This example may seem extreme. It usually does not take a marching band and an elephant to make staff members feel appreciated. In a school district in New York, for example, a high school math teacher who was being trained to implement cooperative learning was observed by the assistant principal. The math teacher conducted a cooperative lesson. The assistant principal wrote up a summary of the lesson and told the principal how impressive the lesson was. The principal then told the superintendent how effective the teacher was in conducting a cooperative lesson. The superintendent wrote the math teacher a letter, congratulating the teacher on conducting an excellent cooperative learning lesson. The math teacher was impressed. He stated that in 25 years of teaching, this was the first time he had received a letter of any kind from a superintendent.

What makes a difference to each individual staff member is to know that his or her successes are perceived, recognized, and celebrated. Leaders search out "good news" opportunities and orchestrate celebrations of how well cooperative learning is being implemented in the school.

Striving for increased instructional expertise is an arduous and long-term enterprise. Teachers become exhausted, frustrated, and disenchanted. They often are tempted to give up. **Leaders must inspire teachers to continue the journey by encouraging the heart** (Kouzes & Posner, 1987). Leaders inspire staff members by giving them the courage and hope to continue the quest. This does not require elephants and marching bands (although they are not a bad idea). What it does require is:

1. The recognition of individual contributions to the common vision.

2. Frequent group celebrations of individual and joint accomplishments.

Staff members do not start the day with a desire to fail. It is the principal's job to show them that they can succeed. **The primary tools for doing so are individual recognition and group celebration.** A leader becomes a master of celebration. Leaders should give out stickers, t-shirts, buttons, and every other conceivable award when staff members achieve a milestone. One leader sends out cards that have "I heard something good about you" printed at the top. Hard work can also be fun work. Hoopla is important to committed efforts. **Leaders find ways to celebrate accomplishments.** If you do not show your appreciation to your staff members, they are going to stop caring, and then, in essence, you are going to find yourself out of business.

To give individual recognition and have a group celebration requires a cooperative organizational structure. In competitions, to declare one person a winner is to declare all others losers. Group celebrations do not take place in competitive / individualistic organizations. In such environments, praise may be perceived to be phony or satirical and recognition may be the source of embarrassment and anxiety about future retaliation by colleagues. **Within cooperative enterprises, however, genuine acts of caring draw people together and forward. Love of teaching, students, and each other is what inspires many staff members to commit more and more of their energy to their jobs.** Consider Dave Joyner's description of the Penn State football team and its coach, Joe Paterno:

> *"The reason we were so good, and continued to be so good, was because he (Joe Paterno) forces you to develop an inner love among the players. It is much harder to give up on your buddy, than it is to give up on your coach. I really believe that over the years the teams I played on were almost unbeatable in tight situations. When we needed to get that six inches we got it because of our love for each other. Our camaraderie existed because of the kind of coach and kind of person Joe was."*

Establishing a cooperative structure and encouraging the development of caring and committed relationships among staff members may just be the best-kept secret of exemplary leadership.

Leaping The Abyss Of Failure

"When you look into the abyss, the abyss is looking into you."

Nietzsche

Teachers travel on the path of the status quo. At the end of the path lies long-term failure through trying to educate students with obsolete and outdated teaching strategies and procedures. Adherents to the status quo slowly and gradually descend into the abyss. They are descending even though they may not always realize it. Along side of the path is the abyss of failure. On the other side of the abyss is increased professional expertise. To improve their professional expertise, teachers must choose to risk failure in the short-term by experimenting with new and different instructional strategies and procedures and by refining and improving their competencies as a teacher. Each time they use a new teaching strategy they take a leap over the abyss of failure to reach enhanced expertise. Sometimes their leap falls short and they fail. Sometimes they soar high above the abyss to land safely on the other side. Sometimes they choose to not leap at all but to travel safe and secure on the path of the status quo. **Managers organize the easy walk downward along the path of the status quo. Leaders encourage and inspire teachers to take the difficult leaps toward increased competence.**

Summary

How effective your school is depends on the psychological and physical energy teachers are willing to commit to educating students. The commitment of teachers, in turn, often depends on whether the principal is a manager or a leader. Managers handle the status quo. Leaders take teachers and other staff members on a journey toward increased professional expertise. Leaders inspire staff members to have the courage to risk short-term failure in order to increase their expertise in the long-term. Teachers must have the courage to leave the status quo of competitive/individualistic classroom strategies and procedures and experiment with cooperative learning. Leading teachers to increased instructional expertise requires the principal to be a leader to challenge the status quo of competitive/individualistic tradition, inspire a vision of what the school could be if cooperative learning were used frequently and consistently, organize teachers into cooperative teams (e.g., colleagial support groups, task forces, and ad hoc decision-making groups), model the use of cooperative procedures, and encourage staff members to have the heart to continue their quest to be better and better teachers.

The most important aspect of providing leadership is organizing staff members into cooperative teams. Three types of cooperative teams are necessary: colleagial support groups to encourage and support each other's efforts to use cooperative learning, task forces to make recommendations about how to deal with school-wide issues such as curriculum revision and communication with parents, and ad hoc decision-making groups to involve all staff members in the important school decisions. This is not an easy task due to the "loosely structured" nature of the school as an organization. It is to the issue of organizational structure that we turn in the next chapter.

Cooperative Skills

Forming . . .

1. Move into groups without noise and bothering others.
2. Stay with the group.
3. Use quiet voices.
4. Encourage everyone to participate.
5. Use names, look at the speaker, no "put-downs," keep hands and feet to oneself.

Functioning . . .

1. Direct group's work (state and restate purpose of assignment; provide time limits; offer procedures.
2. Express support and acceptance verbally and nonverbally.
3. Ask for help or clarification.
4. Offer to explain or clarify.
5. Paraphrase others' contributions.
6. Energize the group.
7. Describe feelings when appropriate.

Formulating . . .

1. Summarize out loud as completely as possible.
2. Seek accuracy by correcting and/or adding to summaries.
3. Seek elaboration.
4. Seek clever ways of remembering ideas and facts.
5. Demand vocalization.
6. Ask other members to plan out loud how they would teach the material.

Fermenting . . .

1. Criticize ideas, not people.
2. Differentiate when there is disagreement within the group.
3. Integrate different ideas into a single position.
4. Ask for justification on conclusions or answers.
5. Extend other members' answers.
6. Probe by asking in-depth questions.
7. Generate further answers.
8. Test reality by checking the group's work.

Chapter 2

Leading A Loosely Coupled Organization

"The Status Quo" Versus "What We Could Be"

Schools are sites for an inevitable and eternal conflict. On one side are the **forces of maintenance and continuity**, which **strive to create and sustain the use of orderly and predictable educational procedures**. Opposing them are the **forces of innovation and discontinuity**, which **seek to alter established practices**. Both seek the same goal of ensuring that students are well educated. Both are needed. The creative tension between the two is what powers considered and thoughtful development and change.

These same two forces operate within the individual staff member. Teachers will experience the conflict between the security of the past and the satisfactions of new professional growth and accomplishment. Each teacher may choose to relate to and instruct students by relying on the established modes of the past or to experiment with new patterns of behavior and thereby change him- or herself. The status quo side wants to continue what he or she has done in the past. Often the track record of the past behavior is good. "If 90 percent of my students score in the top 25 percent of the

SAT's," a high school English teacher said to us, "why should I change the way I teach?" The enhanced expertise side strives for growth, change, and increased competence. **Leaving the status quo and risking one's current success against the potential of being even better in the future requires courage.**

Every staff member with authority is faced with the choice between managing the status quo and providing leadership to create a better and more effective school. In making the choice between being a leader and a manager, individuals must assess the short- and long-term risks of failure. **Leading** involves a short-term risk of failure as staff members experiment with new professional strategies and procedures and a long-term promise of success as the professional expertise of staff members increases. **Managing** promises short-term safety and a long-term promise of failure as professional practices become outdated and obsolete. The short- and long-term risks of failure are at the heart of the conflict between "the status quo" and "what the school could be."

There is an ancient saying that **a journey begins with a single step**. Convincing teachers to take the first step in increasing their expertise is not as easy as it sounds. Leaving the status quo and striking out in a new direction creates anxiety. The anxiety is based on feelings of helplessness and a fear of failure and humiliation.

The status quo, what the teacher currently does, provides security. There is short-term safety in the continued use of current professional strategies and procedures. Change typically involves anxiety. **When faced with that anxiety, many teachers follow the rule of the status quo: In doubt? Do what you did yesterday. If it is not working, do it twice as hard, twice as fast, and twice as carefully!** But the need to increase one's expertise, to become more competent, and to grow and develop professionally, forces staff members to change their professional strategies and procedures. **Growth involves the risk of short-term failure and helplessness.** Anxiety is then experienced. "Will this make me look foolish in front of my class" and "What do I say if students challenge the new procedures" are questions reflecting the anxiety teachers feel when asked to use new instructional strategies. Whenever there is a basic change in teaching strategies, in relationships with students and colleagues, or within one's self, teachers will be anxious about potential failure and helplessness in a changed world.

The developmental problem is how teachers can increase their professional competence while retaining the security of the status quo. Professional growth and change pose a threat to their professional identify because growth demands the abandonment of past securities in the short-term and promises a more satisfying professional identity and more secure professional relationships in the future. Change and growth are exciting, appealing, and inevitable, but they produce anxiety about losing the security of being what one now is. To grow professionally, staff members must abandon the security of past practices.

To summarize:

1. **The motivation to grow and develop professionally** is based on the attraction of novelty, innate human curiosity, the pleasures and satisfactions of competence, the need for new intellectual challenges, and changing social demands. These forces push toward professional development, increasing one's professional competence, and better understanding oneself, one's professional relationships with others, and one's place in the school and the community. Striving to grow professionally requires experimenting with new strategies and procedures, risking short-term failure in order to increase long-term effectiveness, and coping with the resulting short-term anxiety.

2. **Resistance to change** is based on the security of the known, the tendency for the self once structured to perpetuate itself, and the anxiety of separation. Maintaining the status quo is safe and secure in the short-run, but creates inevitable long-term professional failure and ineffectiveness.

3. In doing their jobs, **staff members are faced with numerous demands, opportunities, and challenges** and must deal with them by either relying on the established modes of the past or by trying new strategies and procedures and, in the process, change themselves professionally and personally.

4. Whether staff members choose to stick with the status quo or attempt to grow professionally is a **personal choice involving risk, anxiety, and courage.** Whether staff members choose to increase their professional expertise or cling to the past depends in large part on the encouragement, support, and acceptance they receive from the principal and peers. The lower the support and acceptance a staff members feels, the more likely he or she will be to cling inappropriately to past procedures and strategies. It takes a colleagial support system to provide these teachers with the security and support they need to risk changing their instructional practices.

For schools to be effective, teachers must have the courage to strive to increase their professional expertise continually. They must take the risk of experimenting with new teaching practices in order to progressively improve their instructional competence. **Leaders create a school climate in which teachers have the courage to challenge their current instructional practices and try to grow and develop professionally.**

Through challenging, inspiring, empowering, modeling, and encouraging, leaders seek to maximize the commitment of teachers to grow and develop professionally and give them the courage to seek to increase their instructional expertise daily. The major barrier to that commitment and courage is the "loosely coupled" nature of the school and the resulting competitive / individualistic orientation of most staff members. That barrier is overcome by organizing staff members into cooperative teams.

Change is unlikely when the status quo is unquestioned. Dissatisfaction with existing instructional methods and teacher-teacher relationships is necessary for change to occur. Leaders are pioneers who are willing to take risks to innovate and experiment to find new and better ways of instructing students. To do so requires them to challenge the effectiveness of the status quo. Maintaining the status quo breeds mediocrity. It guarantees long-term failure through obsolescence and atrophy. In order to challenge the status quo leaders must recognize it and realize that a better alternative exists. The status quo may be challenged on two levels. The first level is the organizational structure of the school and the second level is the instructional methods used in the classroom.

Organizing staff members into colleagial support groups, task forces, and ad hoc decision-making groups is not an easy process due to the traditional loosely coupled organizational structure existing within schools and the consequent competitive / individualistic orientation of the faculty and staff. The isolation of staff members from each other and the low-level and amorphous competitive orientation that results reduces their commitment to instructional success and courage to strive to increase their professional expertise. In order to challenge the current organizational structure of the school, leaders must have a basic understanding of the school as an organization, the loosely coupled nature of the school, and the alternative organizational structures that may be implemented.

The School As An Organization

"Everyone has to work together; if we can't get everybody working toward common goals, nothing is going to happen."

Harold K. Sperlich, President, Chrysler Corporation

The **school** is above all else a social organization made up of a network of interpersonal relationships structured to facilitate the achievement of established goals. Schools are **not** buildings, machines, and curriculum. **Schools are relationships and interactions among people.**

The **productivity of the school** primarily depends on (1) the psychological and physical energy students, teachers, and other staff members are willing to commit to their work, and (2) staff members' ability to work together cooperatively to achieve the school's goals. The greater the amount of physical and psychological energy members commit, and the more effective they are in working together to achieve mutual goals, the greater their productivity. The five organizational requirements to ensure the productivity of the school are:

1. Know what their mission and goals are. A school must have clear, cooperative goals that personnel are committed to achieve.

2. A network of interpersonal relationships structured by role definitions and norms defining appropriate behavior. Staff members must be organized into cooperative groups (i.e., colleagial support groups, task groups, and ad hoc decision-making groups). Teacher commitment and expertise are built out of a cooperative structure, not from just having "good" teachers. Individual brilliance or personality are **not** responsible for productiveness. It takes leadership to **get extraordinary effort from ordinary people.**

3. Have the instructional expertise (i.e., skills and attitudes) required to educate students.

4. Have the interpersonal and small group skills required to function effectively as part of colleagial support and decision-making groups.

5. Be effectively managed so that the available human and material resources are organized into a total system for achieving the school's goals.

The school can be described as an **open system** consisting of inputs, a transformational process, and outputs. The school **inputs** (1) students and (2) personnel, materials, buildings, and information. The latter are used to **transform** the students into **outputs** of socialized, skilled, trained, and healthy members of society who enter other organizations such as colleges, corporations, families, and communities. From this point of view, **a school is a recurring pattern of interpersonal interactions within which inputs are transformed into outputs.** All this is portrayed in Figure 1.1.

Figure 1.1
The School As An Open System:
Flow of Materials, Energy, And Information

Inputs	Transformation	Outputs
That which is	Educational goals	Socialized,
transformed:	Roles and norms	skilled, trained,
Students	Technology	healthy
That which does	Management	members
the transforming:		of society.
Personnel, Mat-		
erials, Building.		

Organizations are either growing/improving or declining.
There is no "steady state." To grow and improve, organizations
must adapt their transformation processes to the changes in the inputs they receive, the environment in which they function, and the
outputs they wish to produce. Similar to gaining expertise, being
productive as a school is a process rather than a product. Schools
need to become more productive continually, rather than resting
on their laurels. Being productive involves changing the transformation process to adapt to changes in the students entering the
school, the requirements of society for school graduates, and new
understandings of effective teaching and instruction. As students
change, so should teaching methods. As society changes, and new
competencies and attitudes are required of citizens, the ways
teachers instruct students also need to change. As research continues on how to instruct students most effectively, teaching practices also need to change. Adapting the transformational process
to the inputs received, the outputs required, and the available transformation technologies is one way to view organizational effectiveness.

In order to adapt the tranformation process to the inputs
received and the outputs required, there must be management and,
hopefully, leadership. **Managing** is the process of coordinating the
efforts of staff members to achieve the school's mission and goals.
Managers do not promote change. They manage what exists and
leave things pretty much as they found them when they move on.
Leading is about change, innovation, and enhanced expertise.
These are not the provinces of lonely, half-mad individuals with
flashes of genius. Rather, it is a learned, systematic, purposeful,
and organized search for changes to improve the effectiveness of
the school. Innovation and change do not occur through the
idiosyncratic behavior of charismatic genius. Rather innovation
and change are created by progressing in a disciplined way through
the five leadership steps. Leaders are individuals who are not afraid
to challenge the status quo, who inspire staff members to risk short-
term failure for long-term enhanced expertise, who create cooperative structures within which staff members become committed to
each other's success and care about each other as people, who
live their values by using cooperative strategies and procedures,

and who encourage staff members to have the heart to persist in striving to increase their expertise each day.

Being a leader is not easy. Frequently, when you try to provide leadership to increase the productiveness of your staff, you run into the "brick wall" of the current loosely coupled school structure. To lead the school you need to understand the current competitive / individualistic school structure, you have to reorganize the staff into cooperative units, and you need to inspire staff to be committed to improve their expertise.

The Loosely Coupled Nature Of The School

There are four fifth-grades in Morningside School, each taught by a single teacher. During the first hour Sue decides to have students work in pairs reading a story in their reading book. Jane conducts a class discussion about a television show most of the class saw the night before. Sam is tired. He has students work on math problems while he gets organized for the day. Frank has a special science project planned to precue a field trip his class will be taking next week. In Morningside School teachers are autonomous, free to plan each day as they see fit. They are expected to finish the math and reading curriculums for the year, but most of the time they only have vague notions of what each other is really doing in his or her classes. This organizational structure is different from what is found within business and industry.

Most business organizations are **tightly coupled**. They have clear coals (such as making a profit producing cars), the members are highly interdependent (one person puts the hinges on the frame, the next person puts the door in place, a third person places pins in the hinges to keep the door in place). Each person is clearly accountable (if the hinges are not in place, it is clear who did not do his or her job). Training in how to interact effectively with subordinates and peers is regularly given to supervisors (this is called management training). A quality control person is appointed to ensure that the whole procedure is regularly reviewed and its effectiveness considered. **This combination of clear goals, high interdependence, clear individual accountability, appropriate social skill training, and group processing is so common that when most people think of an organization they automatically assume that these elements are in place.**

Schools are different. Schools are **loosely coupled** organizations consisting of units, processes, actions, and individuals that are typically connected loosely rather than tightly. In a loosely coupled organization the actions generated by one person or unit in the organization bear little predictable relationship to the actions of another person or unit. This means that there is independence rather than interdependence among staff members and schools, processes seem disconnected rather than linked, actions seem isolated from consequences, and staff members function with little or no supervision.

As loosely coupled organizations, schools have a number of **unique characteristics. First**, is **goal ambiguity.** The goals of most schools are ambiguous and to a large extent immeasurable. While the school board may place reading and math achievement as the highest priority, many teachers may place students' self-esteem and higher-level reasoning/critical thinking as their highest priority, and many principals may place students' having a positive attitude toward school and learning as the top priority of schools. Each staff member may have a different set of goals, and a different prioritizing of goals, because of the goal ambiguity existing within most school districts and schools. In addition, the day-to-day role behaviors needed to achieve the school's goals often cannot be specified and, therefore, cannot be measured. To create a **vision** as to what the school can be and what staff members can accomplish, you and they have to be clear about the goals you are seeking to accomplish and how they are prioritized into the school's "mission" by identifying them and ranking them in terms of their importance.

The **second** unique characteristic of schools is **low positive interdependence**. At the building level principals and at the classroom level teachers are more independent from each other than interdependent. Within schools and classrooms, there is a **low division of labor** (so that the actions of one teacher do not directly depend on the previous actions of another teacher), a **low integration of role activities**, and **low joint rewards**. What the teachers (or principals) do, therefore, cannot build momentum and team work cannot be rewarded.

The **third** unique characteristic of schools is **low individual accountability** as role performance is invisible to colleague support and sanction. What one teacher does in his or her own classroom is usually not observed or monitored by other staff members. The **fourth** unique characteristic is that **collaborative skills are de-emphasized**. Teams, therefore, often dissolve from teachers' inability to work together effectively. **Finally**, within most schools there tends to be **no group processing** structured. Staff members rarely discuss how effectively they are working together and how their coordination and teamwork may be improved. Because of these unique organizational characteristics teachers are isolated, their productivity is lowered, and teacher stress increases.

Staff members may strive to achieve a unique set of goals. They may function independently from colleagues. They are largely unaccountable for their actions. Staff members are not required to master the interpersonal and group/organization skills necessary to cooperate effectively with colleagues. And staff members rarely discuss how effectively they are coordinating their efforts. In other words, schools are structured so that staff work individualistically and subtly compete with each other. Teachers may feel proprietary about bulletin-board ideas, special units prepared for their students, and classroom decorations. Teachers may take pride in having the most parents request them. It is not only teachers. Principals have been known to cheat on the standardized testing of their students to outperform other principals in their district and state.

Reversing this individualistic/competitive organizational structure is the key to increasing the productivity of the schools. If you let the competitive / individualistic status quo go on, you limit what is accomplished by the staff and students.

Organizational structure is reversed by organizing teachers into colleagial support groups to improve instruction, task forces to focus on school issues and problems, and ad hoc decision-making groups to ensure the involvement of all faculty in important school issues. You cannot order teachers to cooperate. It has to grow out of their sense of mission and priorities.

The loosely coupled nature of schools as organizations has a number of implications for schools in a state of change. And schools are in a state of change. If schools are not adapting to the following changes, they are in a state of decline and will become increasingly ineffective.

Choosing An Organizational Structure

Two are better than one, because they have a good reward for their toil. For if they fall, one will lift up his fellow; but woe to him who is alone when he falls and has not another to lift him up....And though a man might prevail against one who is alone, two will withstand him. A threefold cord is not quickly broken.

Ecclesiastes 4:9 - 12

It is easy to assume that the existing loosely coupled organizational structure of the schools is the only one possible. The status quo is always justified on the basis of it being the only real alternative. In fact, there are a variety of ways that schools may be structured. Leaders may structure staff relationships competitively, individualistically, or cooperatively. Within schools, staff members may compete with each other to see who is best, work individualistically on their own, or cooperate to achieve the school's goals and accomplish the school's mission.

A **competitive** school structure exists when teachers work against each other to achieve a goal that only one or a few can attain. Within competitive situations there is a negative correlation among staff members' goal attainments, that is, when teachers perceive that they can obtain their goals if and only if the other teachers with whom they are competitively linked fail to achieve their goals. When one runner wins a race, for example, all the other runners in the race lose. Thus, teachers will maximize their own personal gain at their colleagues' expense. Awarding merit pay to the best teacher in the building is an example. By being the best teacher a person deprives all of his or her colleagues from receiving merit pay. Competitors recognize that others' successes threaten and frustrate their own aspirations. The success of teachers is determined by comparing a teacher's performance with the performance of his or her colleagues and distributing rewards on a differential basis with the "best" performances receiving the most and the "worst" performers receiving the least. Thus, within a competitive structure, teachers are expected and encouraged to:

1. Strive for differential benefit (try to be better than their colleagues).

2. Recognize their negatively linked fate (the more one gains, the less for everyone else).

3. Recognize that their rewards are determined both by their own performance **and** the performance of their colleagues (a staff member does not have to be excellent, just better than his or her colleagues).

4. Celebrate the failures and problems of colleagues (their failure increases one's own chances of success).

Staff members are closer to reaching their goals when colleagues perform ineffectively and fail to reach theirs. Staff members may be tempted to mislead others and interfere with others' attempts to teach effectively. Closed to being influenced by colleagues for fear of being exploited, competitors doubt that they can influence others except by coercion and threat. Sabotage of each other's work is a natural result. Productivity and morale typically suffer.

Within many schools there is a diffuse and amorphous competition among teachers without clear rules, with no clear beginning or ending, and unclear criteria for determining winners and losers. In a recent study of teachers, for example, Ashton and Webb (1986) found that most teachers felt isolated from their colleagues, were aware that their colleagues were highly judgmental, believed that the judgments were being made on fragmentary information, and believed that colleagues would not provide help and assistance to solve whatever problems the teachers were facing in their classrooms. Such conditions encouraged teachers to camouflage rather than confront their shortcomings and to exaggerate, to themselves and others, what they took to be their accomplishments. Most teachers worked to create the impression of competence by advertising their achievements, tempering their failures, and concealing their self-doubts. One teacher said that at her school it was well understood that you should "never let another teacher find a weakness or an area you need help in." She went on to say, "You can never go into a teachers' lounge and hear a teacher say, 'Damn, I really failed that kid today.' You never hear that. You always hear how a teacher was on top of a situation." A teacher stated that outright bragging about your competence was unwise. She stated, "Other teachers don't like that. Don't brag, because we are all competitors and we all think we're very intelligent."

An **individualistic** school structure exists when teachers work by themselves to accomplish goals unrelated to the goals of other teachers. Within individualistic situations there is no correlation among teachers' goal attainments, that is, when teachers perceive that obtaining their goal is unrelated to the goal achievement of colleagues. A person's success in swimming fifty yards, for example, is unrelated to whether others swim fifty yards or not. **Theoretically an individualistic school structure is possible, but actually when an individualistic structure is implemented, relations**

among teachers quickly move to competition. At the very least an individualistic structure focuses teachers on strict self-interest and promotes a myopic view of teaching as instructing **my** students in **my** classroom in **my** subject area. Within such a context teachers believe that they are independent from their colleagues, that their rewards are based only on their own performance (e.g., any teacher who achieves a preset criteria for excellence is given merit pay), and that the success or failure of their colleagues has no relevance to one's own professional life.

A **cooperative** school structure exists when teachers coordinate their efforts to achieve joint goals. Within cooperative situations there is a positive correlation among teachers' goal attainments, that is, teachers perceive that they can achieve their goals if and only if the other teachers with whom they are cooperatively linked obtain their goals. When a team of climbers, for example, reaches the summit of a mountain, the success is experienced by all members of the team. In a cooperatively structured school teachers seek outcomes that are beneficial both to themselves and to their colleagues. Joint gain and mutual benefit become the focus of teachers' efforts. Awarding merit pay on the basis of how well all members of the colleagial support group have performed is an example. Being a competent teacher not only increases one's own chances for receiving merit pay but also the chances of one's colleagues. The success of any one teacher is determined by one's own performance **and** the performance of one's colleagues. Rewards are distributed on an "equality" basis with all group members receiving the same merit bonus. Teachers, therefore, accept responsibility for continuously improving (a) their own productivity and (b) the productivity of their colleagues. Cooperative relations among staff members promote:

1. Striving for mutual benefit so that all colleagues benefit from one's efforts.

2. Recognizing that all staff members share a common fate.

3. Recognizing that one's performance is mutually caused by oneself and one's colleagues.

4. Feeling proud and jointly celebrating when a colleague is recognized for professional competence.

There is a myth in our society that the efficiency of work increases when individuals work alone, by themselves, without contact or interaction with others. The more efficient way for work to be structured is assumed to be individualistic or competitive, where every person has their own space, materials, and goals, and works either to outperform their peers or to achieve up to a preset criteria of excellence. Other individuals are viewed as sources of disruption and distraction who lower performance and increase the amount of time necessary to complete the task. The purpose of one's work is to maximize one's own rewards.

The loosely coupled status quo of individual teachers working on their own in diffuse competition with their peers is not working well enough. It should be challenged. There is an alternative that is discussed in depth in the next chapter. Briefly, **if teachers are to be productive, they must interact within a cooperative context.** A clear cooperative structure is the first prerequisite for an effective school. Organizing teachers into small cooperative teams will result in greater productivity and expertise among the teachers, more positive colleagial relationships and cohesion as a staff, greater social support within the faculty, and greater professional self-esteem by more teachers.

Status Quo Of The Classroom: Domination Of Competitive / Individualistic Learning

"I've worked hard, become rich, mean, and friendless. In America, that is about as far as one can go."

Hello Dolly

There is a reciprocal relationship between the instructional methods used in the classroom and the organizational structure of the school. No one should be surprised that when teachers spend their day teaching individualistic and competitive values to students, they themselves will come to believe in such values. There is considerable evidence that people adopt the attitudes and values they espouse to others. The result is that teachers view the school and their job from a competitive perspective and stop thinking of mutual benefit and think only of their own personal benefit, both of which are antithetical to organizational effectiveness.

What is the status quo, the current instructional practices, that teachers must move beyond? During the past 45 years competitive and individualistic learning have dominated, being used from 80 to 93 percent of the time in American schools (Anderson, 1984; Goodlad, 1983; D. Johnson & Johnson, 1976; R. Johnson, 1976; R. Johnson, Johnson, & Bryant, 1973). Within most learning situations students are supposed to listen quietly, read, write answers on worksheets, and hand in reports, without interacting with peers and speaking to the teacher only when invited to do so.

Goodlad (1983) found in an observational study of actual classrooms that teachers who employed a wide variety of learning modes were extremely rare. Teaching was almost exclusively the presentation of information, and learning was nearly always seen as the passive intake of information or as practice. Teachers out-talked their students by a ratio of nearly three to one. And most of this teacher talk consisted of telling--the presentation of information. During the small amount of questioning that took place, fewer than 1/6 of the questions were open-ended ones requiring students to respond in complex ways. Chances were less than 8 percent that students in these classrooms would be involved in discussion, simulation, role playing, or demonstration. Students worked cooperatively less than 10 percent of the time. Goodlad notes that these classrooms had an emotional climate best described as flat. Teachers expressed little warmth and enthusiasm, encouragement, or praise, and students expressed little eagerness, curiosity, or overtly positive responses (overtly negative behavior was noticeably absent as well).

Lorin Anderson (1984) in a systematic observational study of 153 classrooms in South Carolina found that teachers rarely engaged students in discussions of the students' ideas, perspectives, or opinions. Teachers spent the major portion of the class time talking to students about subjects to be learned, directing short-answer questions to the students, and assigning students work. Moran (1980) notes that teachers tend to speak four times for each student utterance, give very little feedback (positive or negative), provided few advance organizers for students, infrequently checked for students' understanding of instructions, primarily lectured by stating facts and opinions and giving commands, and rarely questioned students. Students were not asked to demonstrate knowledge verbally.

Schumaker, Sheldon-Wildgen, & Sherman (1980) found in junior-high schools that teachers used seatwork (where students worked individualistically on assignments using reading and writing skills) 47 percent of the time, lectured 41 percent of the time, had whole-class discussions 9 percent of the time, and used audio-visual aids 10 percent of the time. Group work and individual reports to the class were practically nonexistent. Doyle (1983), in a review of the existing research, found that between 60 and 70 percent of a student's school day was spent in seatwork.

These and other studies indicate that classrooms are over-whelmingly dominated by lecture, individual seatwork, and com-petitive grading practices. Once these methods of teaching were considered acceptable and even desirable. But no longer. Today the research evidence is clear. Students achieve higher, learn more, use higher-level reasoning strategies more frequently, and retain what they learn longer, when they work together in coopera-tive learning groups than when they participate in competitive or in-dividualistic learning situations (Johnson & Johnson, 1983, in press; Johnson, Maruyama, Johnson, Nelson, & Skon, 1981). Within schools, current instructional practices are markedly discrepant from what research indicates would be the most effective way to in-struct students.

To understand the problems this discrepancy between the status quo of teaching and what research indicates is a more effec-tive instructional practice creates for principals, it may be helpful to review Hans Christian Andersen's tale of **The Emperor's New Clothes**. The tale is about an emperor who invests substantial time and money in order to be well-dressed, largely ignoring his other responsibilities. One day two dishonest men arrive at court. Pretending to be weavers, they claim that they are able to create garments so fine that they are not visible to people who are either unfit for the office that they hold, or stupid. The emperor's vanity and desire to test the competence of his staff leads him to be duped. The weavers are supplied with silk, gold thread, and money, all of which they keep for themselves while pretending to weave the emperor's new clothes.

When the weavers announce that the clothes are ready the emperor sends a succession of trusted ministers to see them. Not wanting to appear unfit for office or stupid, they all report that the new clothes are lovely. Finally, the emperor himself goes to see the clothes which were so heartily praised by his subordinates. Al-though he sees nothing, he proclaims, "Oh! The cloth is beautiful! I am delighted with the clothes!"

On the day of a great procession the emperor disrobes, dons his nonexistent new clothes, and marches through his kingdom, warmed only by the ooh's and ah's emitted by his subjects when they "see" his new clothes. Never before had any of the emperor's clothes caused so much excitement (as we can well imagine). Then, with an innocent persistence, a small child said, "But the emperor has nothing on at all!" The child was not yet constrained by the forces that silenced the adult crowd and caused them, despite the evidence of their senses, to validate their superior's false judgment.

This story is a fine example of events that all too often occur in schools: **Not wanting to appear unfit or stupid, staff members conform to the current consensus and are afraid to challenge the collective judgment of how best to teach.** Mistakes are made and then carried forward by sheer momentum, while almost everyone persists in the hollow pretense that all is well.

How effective is the status quo of competitive and individualistic learning? Many teachers consider it the only alternative. They have no vision of what could be done instead. Yet, as will be covered in Chapter 4, cooperative learning is a viable alternative. Requiring students to be passive, silent, and isolated is directly contradicted by the research on the variables affecting productivity and achievement.

The Changing School

How relevant is the loosely coupled competitive / individualistic organizational structure and the instructional use of competitive and individualistic learning in today's world? Given that schools are social organizations that transform inputs into outputs, the transformation process (essentially, how teachers instruct students and how the the work of staff members is organized) must be continually adapted to take into account changes in the (1) inputs, (2) requirements for outputs, and (3) available transformation technologies. There are two ways inputs have changed: students have changed and teachers have changed. The world, furthermore, is becoming increasingly interdependent with the accelerated pace of technological change, and the competencies and attitudes business and industry requires of workers have changed.

Changes In Students

Since the 1950's, there has been a marked change in the students attending American schools. Today's students are qualitatively different from yesterday's in several ways:

1. In the 1950's 58 percent of American families were "Leave It To Beaver" families with the father working, the mother at home, and two children in school. In 1986 this family configuration applied to only 14 percent of American families. Today it is less than 10 percent.

2. In the 1950's, children were an important part of the economic unit of the family and lived in neighborhoods and communities in which they viewed and interacted with adults at work. Children and adolescents, therefore, were skilled in working cooperatively with others and understood the relationship between education and work. Today, children are not part of the economic unit of the family, housing and work settings are separated, children and adolescents have little experience in working cooperatively, and even lack interpersonal experience as they spend much of their time watching TV.

3. A higher percentage of today's students are "at risk" students who are poor, minority, troubled, non-English speaking, lonely, isolated, and socially unskilled students.

There are many other ways in which students are different today from the 1950's. You may wish to add them to this list. As you do so, remember that if schools are not adapting to the reality that today's students are qualitatively different from yesterday's, their organizational productivity is declining.

Changes In Staff Members

> *"I will pay more for the ability to deal with people than any other ability under the sun."*

John D. Rockefeller

Students are not the only ones who are changing. Teachers, principals, and staff members are becoming older (i.e., the school is graying). Soon, large numbers of new, inexperienced, young staff members will be found in schools. The former group of teachers have functioned for decades in loosely structured schools that promoted a competitive / individualistic orientation among staff members. The latter group has been educated within a competitive / individualistic school environment that may have emphasized an egocentric preoccupation with one's own success at the expense of others. Neither group may be very skilled interpersonally.

Traditionally, teachers have not been skilled in working effectively with adult peers. Blake and Mouton (1974) found that teachers and administrators lacked teamwork skills and were too ready to resolve differences by voting or by following the "official leader." They observed that educators are far less competent in working in small problem-solving groups than industrial personnel. And they found that educators described themselves as being more oriented toward compromising quality of work for harmonious relationships, exerting minimal effort to get their job done, and being more oriented toward keeping good relationships than toward achieving the organization's goals. Blumberg, May, and Perry (1974) found that teachers were ill-equipped behaviorally to function as part of a problem-solving group. They lacked the skills and attitudes needed for effective group problem-solving.

The training of teachers has focused so exclusively on the teacher-pupil relationship that little attention has been given to the skills and attitudes needed to interact with colleagues. Practically none of the energy going into training teachers has been concerned about the school as an organization or learning how to function as an adult peer in the school.

Within a loosely structured organization teachers function independently and are rarely expected to work cooperatively with each other and, therefore, the competencies required to be an effective adult peer are of little consequence. Teachers do not have to have them. When teachers become more interdependent, however, an important responsibility of the principal is to ensure that teachers gain the interpersonal and small group competencies required to work effectively with colleagues. **There are basically two approaches to training teachers to be competent adult peers within a school:**

1. **Direct**: Provide training programs for teachers in interpersonal and small group skills.

2. **Indirect**: Make teachers responsible for instructing students in interpersonal and small group skills. This approach is based on the truism that, "Whoever teaches learns best." The experience of teaching students interpersonal and small group skills will inherently result in teachers mastering the skills.

Education In A Changing World

"In an industrial organization it's group effort that counts. There's really no room for stars in an industrial organization. You need talented people, but they can't do it alone. They have to have help."

John F. Donnelly, President, Donnelly Mirrors

The rapid change in the world highlights the dilemma of all executives: how to maintain stability in their organizations and, at the same time, provide creative adaptation to the changes in the world. These changes are immense. More new knowledge has been developed in the last ten years than in the previous entire history of the human species. With the speed of change the complexity of relationships multiplies. Cooperation must be established among disparate peoples and nations. **Students increasingly live in a world characterized by interdependence, pluralism, conflict, and rapid change.** The world has become multi-boundary with a diversity of worldwide systems in which all people affect and are affected by others across the globe. In addition, the major problems faced by individuals (e.g., contamination of the environment, warming of the atmosphere, world hunger, international terrorism, nuclear war) are increasingly ones that cannot be solved by actions taken only at the national level. Since an important goal of education is to empower students by inculcating a belief that they are able to take effective action to solve problems, giving students frameworks for how to participate effectively in solving global problems and dealing with global issues becomes an important priority. Students need to develop an understanding of how they participate in setting goals, making decisions, and taking action to ensure that they can meet their needs for security, well-being, equity, and productivity. Understanding the nature of interdependent systems and how to operate effectively within them is an essential quality of future citizens.

The magnitude and scope of world interdependence has greatly increased the past 40 years. Global interdependence is reflected in technological, economic, ecological, and political systems. **Technologically**, jet engines and rocketry, transistors and microchips, nuclear fission and fusion, and many other technological advances are rapidly changing life on earth. Technologies know no boundaries. When scientists make a new discovery in one country, it is quickly picked up and utilized in other countries. Through advances in transportation technologies the earth has shrunk in the time it takes to cover distances. The increased ability to transport people and goods throughout the world has fundamentally changed the world's economy. Through advances in communication technologies the earth has expanded in terms of the number of people, places, events, and bits of information that are available to any one person. **Economically**, we depend on other areas of the world to supply many of the raw materials used by our industries and the goods we consume daily. We also depend on other countries to buy our goods and services. Multinational assemblage of goods is common. Foreign investment by multinational corporations, international lending of money, and the buying and selling of foreign currencies has become the rule rather than the exception. When companies close plants in one part of the world new jobs are created in other parts of the world. Rises or declines in interest rates have dramatic implications for debtor countries. Crop failures in one part of the world affect profits of farmers in another part of the world. Such economic interdependence will continue to increase. Students need to be educated accordingly. **Ecologically**, the pollution of one country most often affects the well-being of other countries, the deforestation in one country affects the weather of many other countries, what affects the ecology in one part of the world affects the ecology in other parts of the world. **Politically**, an election in one country often has important implications for the balance of power among the world's superpowers. By politically deciding to vary economic policy, countries can affect the stability of the governments of other countries.

Because of technological, economic, ecological, and political interdependence the solution to most problems cannot be achieved by one country alone. When nations and organizations work together to solve mutual and/or global problems conflict results. Nations disagree about the nature and cause of the problems, have differing values and goals related to outcomes and means, and in how much each should contribute to the problem-solving efforts. How constructively conflicts are resolved becomes the central issue of how well interdependence is managed.

The mission for schools must be derived from our view of the world as it will be like for our students. They will live in a complex, interconnected world in which cultures collide every minute and dependencies limit the flexibility of individuals and nations. Problems have been internationalized. The dividing lines between domestic and international are becoming blurred. Because information flows so freely around so much of the globe, the content of international affairs is now predominantly the internal affairs of other nations; and the content of "domestic politics" is heavy with international impacts and implications.

Johnson & Johnson

School Can Provide Distorted Views Of Work

Much of what students learn in school may be worthless in the real world. Since school teaches lessons about work that are just wrong for survival on the job, students should be prepared for some shocks. **First**, school teaches that success comes from passing objective tests on one's own. School rarely requires students to lead or direct others or even to work cooperatively with others. **Second**, school may create an impression that if students attend class and do minimal work, a promotion is due every year. That is not the case in most jobs.

Third, success in school work comes from focusing on books and lectures; students can get top grades without ever talking with a professor or a classmate. Education is structured to produce technically competent (more or less) and socially naive people. When you put a person who has learned individually for 12 to 16 years into a job that requires leadership, what usually happens is quite predictable. The person does well on the technical aspect of the job but does poorly in getting the team to function at its full potential. When confronted with a less than optimal evaluation, such people often react defensively and with anger. **Fourth**, attendance in class, coming to school on time, and not missing a day of school, are not emphasized as important in many schools. A student who is allowed to graduate with numerous unexcused absences, regular patterns of tardiness, and a history of uncompleted assignments will make a poor employee. **Fifth**, in many schools there is an attitude that it is up to the teacher to motivate the students, make sure they get to class, and are treated fairly. On the job students are expected to take responsibility for their own motivation and work performance.

Sixth, the implicit message about "work" that gets drummed into students' heads from kindergarten through graduate school is that work (a student's job) means performing some task or tasks largely by oneself, even though this is often done with other people present. Because the needed tools are supplied, goals and rules clearly specified, and the grading of performance "objective," securing cooperation from others is not an important issue. It is even sometimes discouraged as "cheating." From kindergarten through graduate school, students can get excellent performance appraisals and yearly promotions, and yet learn virtually nothing about leading others.

In the real world of work, things are altogether different. The heart of most jobs, especially the higher-paying more interesting jobs, is getting others to cooperate, leading others, coping with complex power and influence issues, and helping solve people's problems in working with each other. Paying attention to superiors, colleagues, and subordinates, knowing what their concerns and pressures are, and knowing what they wish to achieve are important aspects of the social sensitivity on the job. Understanding coworkers and being sensitive to their needs and moods is a vital job survival skill. Finally, learning how to develop a power base is important. To get things done you need a power base to help you influence others. A power base comes from knowledge about the company and its customers; having a good reputation within the company; having a good track record of being responsible, reliable, and productive; and having clear-cut achievements.

Millions of technical, professional and managerial jobs today require much more than technical competence and professional expertise. They also require leadership. Individuals will be asked to get things done by influencing a large and diverse group of people (bosses, subordinates, peers, customers, and others), despite lacking much or any formal control over them, and despite their general disinterest in cooperating.

Getting a group of people that one does not control to march in some needed direction is rarely easy. When they are a diverse group, in background, perspective and priorities, it is even harder. Yet this is precisely the skill that many jobs demand, even of relatively low-level employees in project management and other roles, such as executive secretary. The number of people who can handle these jobs effectively is far less than the number of these jobs.

To learn to be a leader students need to be exposed to experiences in school that teach them a willingness to lead, the ability to motivate others to achieve goals, the ability to get decisions implemented, the ability to exercise authority, the ability to develop credibility, the ability to negotiate, represent, and mediate, and a number of other interpersonal skills. Education should address the behaviors and skills that give individuals the capacity to lead.

Some people pick up the lessons of the work place the hard way, through experience. Others never learn, and become bitter and unsuccessful.

Conclusions

The transformation process of the school (i.e., the instructional practices of teachers and the way in which staff members are organized) needs to be under continual revision based on changes in the inputs received (i.e., students, staff, curriculum materials) and the outputs required (i.e., individuals who are both technically and interpersonally competent, understand interdependent systems, can work well with a wide variety of people, can adapt easily to change, and can provide leadership to group efforts). In order to ensure that teachers are committed to and successful in producing such individuals, principals and other administrators must choose an organizational structure for the school carefully.

Commitment To Increased Professional Expertise

"The greatest rewards come only from the greatest commitment."

Arlene Blum, Mountain Climber and Leader, American Women's Himalayan Expedition

The question has to be asked, "How much individual commitment by teachers and students is generated by the competitive / individualistic approach to organizing staff and student work?" **Within loosely coupled organizations, the commitment of each individual teacher is all.** Teachers and other staff members may go through the motions of their jobs, retired in place, without fear of discovery and/or penalty. Providing leadership in schools is first and foremost creating the conditions under which individual staff members will commit physical and psychological energy to their jobs and dedicate themselves to achieve goals that they sincerely believe are important and meaningful.

Commitment cannot be obtained through exercise of authority. In many cases within loosely coupled organizations, the exercise of authority decreases commitment. Under most conditions, pressure creates resistance. Thus, principals need ways to generate greater commitment from staff members. Ways to do so include:

1. **Focusing on changing groups, not individuals.** In loosely coupled organizations, this means that first you must link teachers with each other to create colleagial support groups within which teachers can influence each other. Individuals adopt, and conform to, the norms of reference groups to which one belongs, aspire to belong, and identify with. Reference group norms are powerful influences on attitudes and behavior, provide social support for continuing to hold attitudes and behavior patterns, reinforce recommended attitudes and behaviors and punish deviation, and help teachers resist efforts to change their attitudes and behaviors. It is easier to promote professional growth and development, attitude acquisition, and behavioral change, by changing the norms and values of the groups to which individuals belong than by changing each individual separately.

There is considerable evidence that indicates individuals are more willing to take risks within small groups than they are when they are working alone. Risking short-term failure to achieve long-term enhanced expertise will happen more easily and frequently when faculty are organized in small groups than when they are expected to work on their own.

2. Committing oneself publicly to one's colleagues to take the risks necessary to increase one's instructional expertise and, subsequently, being held accountable by peers to fulfill one's commitments. Publicly saying, "I'm going to do it!" is a powerful influence on one's behavior. Attitudes and commitments to engage in specified behavior patterns that are made public are more likely to be adopted than are those that are private, especially when peers hold one accountable to fulfill one's commitments. **Commitment** may be defined as the binding or pledging of the individual to an act or decision (Kiesler, 1971). To the extent that people act in the absence of coercion, publicly commit themselves to act in front of others, or invest time, money, or personal prestige in an activity, they come to see themselves as believers in that sort of activity and develop a personal interest in it (Aronson, 1978; Wicklund & Brehm, 1976).

The greater the personal willingness to adopt attitudes and behavior patterns, and the more explicit and public the attitudes and behaviors are, the greater are the subsequent reactions to attacks on or support for the attitudes and behaviors (Kiesler, 1971; Pallak, Mueller, Dollar, & Pallak, 1972) and the greater the assumed responsibility for subsequent outcomes (Pallak, Sogin, & VanZante, 1974; Wicklund & Brehm, 1976). When individuals "take a stand" on an issue by committing themselves publicly to an attitude position, the attitude position and the implications of the position may become more salient and less easily denied or forgotten in subsequent situations. Individuals who are more publicly committed to their position are more susceptible to subsequent consonant communications advocating a more extreme position, are more resistant to an attack on their position, and are more likely to comply with a subsequent request for additional attitude-related behavior than individuals only privately committed to their position (Halverson & Pallak, 1978; Pallak, Mueller, Dollar, & Pallak, 1972; Sullivan & Pallak, 1976).

The classic studies by Lewin (1943) and his associates (Radke & Klishurich, 1947; Radke & Caso, 1948; Willerman, 1943) on persuading Americans to eat foods they did not ordinarily consume indicate that if you wish to change individuals' attitudes and behavior:

a. They should be involved in group discussions that lead to public commitment to the new attitudes and behaviors.

b. They should perceive that all members of the group support the new attitudes and behaviors. The influence of public commitment on attitudes and behavior patterns is considerably strengthened when group members hold individuals accountable to fulfill their commitments.

3. **Being exposed to visible and credible social models.** Discussions with visible and credible positive models are powerful influences on attitudes and behaviors. Visible and credible models who demonstrate the recommended attitudes and behavior patterns and who directly discuss their importance are powerful influences (Johnson, 1979; Watson & Johnson, 1972). People are most likely to accept new attitudes and behaviors when they come into contact with others who have successfully adopted them (Aronson & O'Leary, 1982-83; Goldman, 1940; Nisbett, Borgida, Crandall, & Reed, 1976; Rogers & Shoemaker, 1971). Visible and credible models and discussion with others who have already adopted the new attitudes and behaviors may be important aspects of trying new teaching practices.

4. **Being confronted with vivid and personalized appeals to try new teaching procedures and expand one's teaching expertise.** Statistical data summaries and impersonal information sources are less vivid than face-to-face discussions. New teaching practices need to be discussed, face-to-face, in ways that make clear how their use fits in with one's current teaching practices and professional identity. "This fits with you!" "Here is why you will like it." are more powerful appeals than is "research says..." People tend to weigh information in proportion to its vividness (Borgida & Nisbett, 1977; Hamill, Wilson, & Nisbett, 1980; Nisbett, Borgida, Crandall, & Reed, 1976; Taylor & Thompson, 1982). Statistical data

summaries and impersonal information sources are less vivid than face-to-face interactions and case studies. Impersonal data summaries, though accurate and efficient, have been shown to have less impact on attitudes and behavior than does more concrete information, even when the more vivid information is less representative. Thus, in order to have maximal impact on learning, attitudes, and behavior, nutrition information needs to be discussed, face-to-face, in ways that make clear the personal implications of the information.

5. **Teaching what they have learned about a new teaching practice to colleagues.** People learn things better if they learn it in order to teach someone else (Allen, 1976; Benware, 1975; Gartner, Kohler, & Riessman, 1971). Higher level conceptual understanding and reasoning are promoted when participants have to teach each other a common way to think about problem situations (Johnson & Johnson, 1979, 1983; Murray, 1983). The way people conceptualize material and organize it cognitively is markedly different when they are learning material for their own benefit and when they are learning material to teach to others (Annis, 1983; Bargh & Schul, 1980; Murray, 1983). Material learned to be taught is learned at a higher conceptual level than is material learned for one's own use. Peers are frequently able to teach more effectively than specially trained experts (Fisher, 1969; Sarbin, 1976).

6. **Advocating new instructional practices to colleagues increases one's commitment to use the practices oneself.** Besides saying, "You should try this!", a teaching practice can be advocated through demonstrations, coplanning lessons, coteaching lessons, and trading curriculum units. People are particularly prone to increase their commitment to teaching practices that they have attempted to persuade another to adopt (Nel, Helmreich, & Aronson, 1969).

What's Next

The first step of leadership is challenging the status quo. The status quo is the loosely coupled competitive / individualistic structure of the school and the domination of competitive / individualistic instruction in the classroom. In order to determine how effective the status quo is, it must be compared against the changing nature of students, staff, society, and world and its ability to generate long-term, persistent, committed efforts by staff and students.

Challenging the status quo, however, is not enough. A vision of what the school could and should be must be presented to focus staff members' attention on what changes they need to make in how they instruct students and how they work together. A requirement for the mutual vision is that it be realistic, that is, concretely based on a validated theory. In the next chapter the research comparing the efficacy of cooperative, competitive, and individualistic efforts will be covered.

RESEARCH REVIEW

Higher achievement
Increased retention
Greater use of higher level reasoning
Increased perspective taking
Greater intrinsic motivation
More positive heterogeneous relationships
Better attitudes toward school
Better attitudes toward teachers
Higher self-esteem
Greater social support
More positive psychological adjustment
More on-task behavior
Greater collaborative skills

Chapter 3

Research On Cooperative Efforts

The Vision: A Cooperative School

"I never got very far until I stopped imagining I had to do everything myself."

Frank W. Woolworth

A leader has to have a vision of what the school could and should be, communicate the vision with commitment and enthusiasm, make it a shared vision that staff members adopt as their own, and make it a rational vision based on theory, research, and solid implementation procedures. The leader is the **keeper of the dream** who inspires commitment to work hard toward actualizing a common vision. It is the common vision that creates a basic sense of "sink or swim together" (i.e., positive interdependence) among staff members and students.

Every excellent school begins with a dream shared by most staff and students. The dream of a cooperative school is that the school will be a place where individuals share, help, encourage, and support each other's efforts to achieve and be productive. A place where staff and students think of **we** not **me**. Where working together to get the job done creates caring and committed relationships that propel people forward in their mutual search for excellence.

To be a cooperative school, there must be some congruence among classroom, school, and district organizational structure. If the classroom and the district are structured competitively, it will be difficult to structure cooperation at the building level. The more the district and school personnel compete with each other, the harder it will be for the teacher to use cooperative learning. **A consistent and coherent organizational structure is established when teachers use cooperative learning in the classroom, school staff members work in cooperative teams, and the superintendent structures the administrators into cooperative teams.** The support and assistance necessary for students, teachers, and administrators to promote each other's success may then be sustained.

A cooperative school structure begins in the classroom. Teachers typically cannot promote isolation and competition among students all day and be collaborative with colleagues. What is promoted in the instructional situations tends to dominate relationships among staff members. Teachers who spend up to six hours a day telling students, "Do not copy," "I want to see what you can do, not your neighbor," "Let's see who is best," and "Who is the winner," will in turn tend to approach their colleagues with the attitudes of, "Don't copy from me," and "Who is the winner in implementing this new teaching strategy." The cooperative context that is necessary for teachers to learn from their colleagues begins in the classroom. Teachers may be expected to (Johnson & F. Johnson, 1987; Johnson, Johnson, & Holubec, 1986):

1. Structure the majority of learning situations cooperatively. Cooperative learning requires that the teacher carefully creates positive interdependence, face-to-face promotive interaction, individual accountability, social skills, and group processing. Each of these elements will be explained in Chapter 4.

2. Teach students the leadership, decision-making, communication, trust-building, and conflict-resolution skills they need to function effectively within cooperative learning groups.

The best way to train teachers in how to function effectively within staff teams may be to train them to use cooperative learning within their classes and to teach their students collaborative skills.

The second level in creating a cooperative school is to form colleagial support groups, task forces, and ad hoc decision-making groups within the school. The interaction among staff members should be as carefully structured as is the cooperative interaction among students in the classroom. All staff members should be involved in groups that meet regularly and work on meaningful tasks.

The third level in creating a cooperative school is to implement administrative cooperative teams within the district. The superintendent should organize the district administrators into cooperative teams similarly to how teachers organize students into cooperative groups. All administrators should be involved in cooperative teams that meet regularly and work on meaningful tasks.

A Rational Vision

In order to be compelling, a vision must be rational. The degree to which a vision is rational depends on whether it is based on a coherent theory that is validated by research and translated into useful implementation procedures. The more carefully constructed the theory and the greater the amount of research testing it, the more rational the vision. A valid theory, however, is incomplete unless the procedures are developed to operationalize it within the classroom and school.

The first question to ask about a vision is, "How rational is it?" At one time educators were convinced that competition among students would create wonderful educational effects. Later educators became convinced that individualistic learning would result in great educational advances. Yet the basic, fundamental aspect of human achievement is cooperation. What is the evidence comparing the effectiveness of cooperative, competitive, and individualistic efforts?

What Do We Know About Cooperative Learning?

Business and industry leaders are rediscovering a basic truth that has escaped educators for the past 30 years (Johnson, Johnson, & Holubec, 1988; Kouzes & Posner, 1987). They have rediscovered that long-term, persistent, committed effort to achieve is powered by caring and committed personal relationships (not tangible rewards or intellectual rationales). When asked about their success, the chief executives of the companies that have the best track records in North America state that they have been successful because they care about their people, not just as employees, but as human beings and as friends. Not only is their personal caring apparent to employees, but the chief executives are able to create teams in which members care about each other on a personal as well as professional level. The successful chief executives create a "family" within which members care deeply about each other and the mutual vision they are striving to actualize. **It is genuine acts of caring that draw people together and move them forward.**

It is time for educators to discover the same "truth." Working together to get the job done can have profound effects on students and staff members. A great deal of research has been conducted on the relationship among cooperative, competitive, and individualistic efforts and instructional outcomes (Johnson & Johnson, 1974, 1975, 1978, 1983, in press; Johnson, Johnson, & Maruyama, 1983; Johnson, Maruyama, Johnson, Nelson, & Skon, 1981; Pepitone, 1980; Sharan, 1980; Slavin, 1983). These research studies began in the late 1890's when Triplett (1897) in the United States, Turner (1889) in England, and Mayer (1903) in Germany conducted a series of studies on the factors associated with competitive performance. The amount of research that has been conducted since is staggering. During the past 90 years over 500 studies have been conducted by a wide variety of researchers in different decades, with different age subjects, in different subject areas, and in different settings. We know far more about the efficacy of cooperative learning than we know about lecturing, age grouping, beginning reading instruction at age six, departmentalization, or almost any other facet of education. While there is not space enough in this chapter to review all of the research, a comprehensive review of all studies may be found in Johnson and Johnson (in press). In most cases, references to individual studies are not included in this chapter. Rather, the reader is referred to reviews that contain the references to the specific studies that corroborate the point being made.

Building on the theorizing of Kurt Lewin and Morton Deutsch, the premise may be made that the type of interdependence structured among individuals determines how they interact with each other which, in turn, results in different outcomes (Johnson & Johnson, in press). By structuring positive interdependence among individuals a promotive interaction pattern characterized by help, assistance, accountability, and encouragement is created, which in turn promotes outcomes such as achievement/productivity, higher-level reasoning and problem solving, positive interpersonal relationships, self-esteem, and social skills.

Interaction Patterns

Simply placing students near each other and allowing interaction to take place does not mean that high quality peer relationships will result and that learning will be maximized. The nature of interaction is important. Some interaction leads to students rejecting each other and defensively avoiding being influenced by peers. When student-student interaction leads to relationships characterized by perceived support and acceptance, then the potential effects described in the previous section are likely to be found.

There have been several hundred studies comparing the effects of cooperative, competitive, and individualistic goal structures on aspects of interpersonal interaction important for learning (see Johnson & Johnson, in press). A cooperative goal structure, that is, positive interdependence among students' learning goals, leads to a promotive interaction pattern among students. **Promotive interaction** may be defined as individuals encouraging and facilitating each other's efforts to achieve. It is characterized by personal and academic acceptance and support, exchange of information, mutual help and assistance, high intrinsic achievement motivation, and high emotional involvement in learning.

A competitive goal structure (i.e., negative interdependence among students' learning goals) results in an oppositional pattern of student-student interaction. **Oppositional interaction** may be defined as individuals discouraging and obstructing each other's efforts to achieve. It results in rejection of classmates, obstruction of each other's work, avoidance of information exchange or communication, low achievement motivation, and psychological withdrawal and avoidance. The negative interdependence created by a competitive goal structure results in students having a vested interest in obstructing one another's learning. There are two ways to win in a competition-- to do better than anyone else or to prevent anyone else from doing better than you. This is known as a good offense and a good defense. In a classroom, however, defending against classmates learning more than you can create destructive interaction patterns that decrease learning for everyone.

An individualistic goal structure (i.e., no interdependence among students' learning goals) results in no interaction among students. **No interdependence** exists when individuals work independently without any interchance with each other. Students work alone without bothering their classmates. Such a goal structure minimizes peer relationships and interaction in learning situations.

Promotive Versus Oppositional Versus No Interaction

Within cooperative learning situations students benefit from helping each other learn, while in competitive learning situations students suffer from obstructing and frustrating each other's learning, and in individualistic learning situations neither encouragement nor opposition takes place. There is considerably more helping, encouraging, tutoring, and assisting among students in cooperative than in competitive or individualistic learning situations (Johnson & Johnson, in press).

Acceptance, Support, Trust, Liking

Cooperative learning experiences, compared with competitive and individualistic ones, have been found to result in stronger beliefs that one is liked, supported, and accepted by other students, and that other students care about how much one learns and want to help one learn (Johnson & Johnson, in press). Furthermore, cooperative attitudes are related to the belief that one is liked by other students and wants to listen to, help, and do schoolwork with other students. Individualistic attitudes are related to **not** wanting to do schoolwork with other students, **not** wanting to help other students learn, **not** valuing being liked by other students, and **not** wanting to participate in social interaction. Furthermore, Deutsch (1962) and other researchers (Johnson, 1974) found that trust is built through cooperative interaction and is destroyed through competitive interaction.

From Table 3.1 it may be seen that cooperation results in greater social support than do competitive or individualistic efforts (effect sizes of 0.47 and 0.87 respectively). Social support is related to (see Johnson & Johnson, in press):

1. Achievement, successful problem solving, persistence on challenging tasks under frustrating conditions, lack of cognitive interference during problem solving, lack of absenteeism, academic and career aspirations, more appropriate seeking of assistance, retention, job satisfaction, high morale, and greater compliance with regimens and behavioral patterns that increase health and productivity.

2. Living a longer life, recovering from illness and injury faster and more completely, and experiencing less severe illnesses.

3. Psychological health and adjustment, lack of neuroticism and psychopathology, reduction of psychological distress, coping effectively with stressful situations, self-reliance and autonomy, a coherent and integrated self-identity, greater psychological safety, higher self-esteem, increased general happiness, and increased interpersonal skills.

4. Effective management of stress by providing the caring, information, resources, and feedback individuals need to cope with stress, by reducing the number and severity of stressful events in an individual's life, by reducing anxiety, and by helping one appraise the nature of the stress and one's ability to deal with it constructively.

5. The emotional support and encouragement individuals need to cope with the risk that is inherently involved in challenging one's competence and striving to grow and develop.

The importance of social support has been ignored within education over the past 30 years. **A general principle to keep in mind is that the pressure to achieve should always be matched with an equal level of social support.** Challenge and support

must be kept in balance. Whenever increased d
sure to be productive are placed on students (an
responding increase in social support should be

Exchange of Information

The seeking of information, and utilizing it in one's learning, is essential for academic achievement. In problem-solving situations, students working within a cooperative goal structure seek significantly more information from each other than do students working within a competitive goal structure (Crawford & Haaland, 1972). Students working within a cooperative goal structure tend to make optimal use of the information provided by other students, whereas students working within a competitive goal structure often fail to do so (Laughlin & McGlynn, 1967). Blake and Mouton (1961) found that competition biases a person's perceptions and comprehension of viewpoints and positions of other individuals. A cooperative context, compared with a competitive one, promotes more accurate communication of information, more verbalization of ideas and information, more attentiveness to others' statements, and more acceptance of and willingness to be influenced by others' ideas and information (Deutsch, 1973; Johnson, 1974). Furthermore, a cooperative context results in fewer difficulties in communicating with and understanding others, more confidence in one's own ideas and in the value that others attach to one's ideas, more frequent open and honest communication, and greater feelings of agreement between oneself and others (Deutsch, 1973; Johnson, 1974; Johnson & Johnson, in press).

Motivation

Motivation is most commonly viewed as a combination of the perceived likelihood of success and the perceived incentive for success. The greater the likelihood of success and the more important it is to succeed, the higher the motivation. Success that is intrinsically rewarding is usually seen as being more desirable for learning than is having students believe that only extrinsic rewards are worthwhile. There is greater perceived likelihood of success and success is viewed as more important in a cooperative than in a competitive or individualistic learning situation (Johnson & Johnson, in press).

The more cooperative students' attitudes, the more they see themselves as being intrinsically motivated: They persevere in pursuit of clearly defined learning goals; believe that it is their own efforts that determine their school success; want to be good students and get good grades; and believe that ideas, feelings, and learning new ideas are important and enjoyable. These studies also indicate that the more competitive students' attitudes are, the more they see themselves as being extrinsically motivated in elementary and junior high schools. Competitive attitudes are, however, somewhat related to intrinsic motivation, to being a good student, and to getting good marks in senior high school. Individualistic attitudes tend to be unrelated to all measured aspects of the motivation to learn. Being part of a cooperative learning group has been found to be related to a high subjective probability of academic success and continuing motivation for further learning by taking more advanced courses in the subject area studied. There is also experimental evidence which indicated that cooperative learning experiences, compared with individualistic ones, will result in more intrinsic motivation, less extrinsic motivation, and less need for teachers to set clear goals for the students.

Emotional Involvement in Learning

Students are expected to become involved in instructional activities and to benefit from them as much as possible. There is evidence that the more cooperative students' attitudes are, the more they express their ideas and feelings in large and small classes and listen to the teacher, whereas competitive and individualistic attitudes are unrelated to indices of emotional involvement in instructional activities. There is evidence that cooperative learning experiences, compared with competitive and individualistic ones, result in a greater desire to express one's ideas to the class. Cooperative learning experiences, compared with competitive and individualistic ones, promote greater willingness to present one's answers and thus create more positive feelings toward one's answers and the instructional experience, as well as more positive attitudes toward the instructional tasks and subject areas.

Cooperative Efforts And Achievement / Productivity

> "The highest and best form of efficiency is the spontaneous cooperation of a free people."

Woodrow Wilson

How successful competitive, individualistic, and cooperative efforts are in promoting productivity and achievement is the first question pragmatists ask about social interdependence. And they have been asking this question for some time. The investigation of the relative impact of the three types of social interdependence on achievement is the longest standing research tradition within American social psychology. It began with a research study by Triplett in 1897 and has extended over 90 years. At least 352 studies with 1,691 findings on productivity and achievement have been conducted. And that does not count the research on social facilitation and other related areas where implicit competition may be found. This represents a major effort within American social sciences. We know more about the relative impact of competitive, individualistic, and cooperative efforts on achievement than we do about almost any other aspect of educational practice.

As with all other areas of social science research, the number of studies conducted in the last 30 years has exploded. Of the 352 studies conducted, 90 percent have been conducted since 1960 and 2/3 have been conducted since 1970. Since research participants have varied widely as to economic class, age, sex, and cultural background, since a wide variety of research tasks and measures of the dependent variables have been used, and since the research has been conducted by many different researchers with markedly different orientations working in different settings and in different decades, the overall body of research on social interdependence has considerable generalizability.

Through meta-analysis procedures the results of the 352 studies may be reduced to a single analysis (Johnson & Johnson, in press). When all of the studies are included in the analysis, the average cooperator performed at about 2/3 a standard deviation above average competitors (effect size = 0.67) and 3/4 a standard deviation above the average person working within an individualistic situation (effect size = 0.67). This means that students at the 50th-percentile in a cooperative learning situation will perform at the 75th-percentile of students learning in a competitive situation and at the 75th-percentile of students learning in an individualistic situation. Students in a competitive learning situation do achieve slightly higher than do students in an individualistic learning situation (effect size = 0.29).

Not all the research, however, has been carefully conducted. The methodological shortcomings found within many research studies may significantly reduce the certainty of the conclusion that cooperative efforts produce higher achievement than do competitive or individualistic efforts. Thus, the results of studies in which students were randomly assigned to conditions, in which there was an unambiguous and well-defined control condition, in which teacher and curriculum effects were controlled for, and in which it was verified that the experimental and control conditions were successfully implemented, were analyzed. When only the high-quality studies were included in the analysis, students at the 50th-percentile of the cooperative learning situation performed at the 81st-percentile of the competitive and individualistic learning situations (effect sizes = 0.86 and 0.88 respectively). Further analyses revealed that the results held constant when group measures of productivity were included as well as individual measures, for short-term as well as long-term studies, and when symbolic as well as tangible rewards were used.

If cooperative learning does in fact promote higher achieve- ment than do competitive and individualistic efforts, it would follow that operationalizations of cooperative learning that contained a mixture of cooperative, competitive, and individualistic efforts would produce lower achievement than would "pure" operationalizations of cooperative learning. The original jigsaw pro- cedure (Aronson, et al., 1978), for example, is a combination of resource interdependence (cooperative) and individual reward structures (individualistic). Teams-Games-Tournaments (DeVries & Edwards, 1974) and Student-Teams-Achievement-Divisions (Slavin, 1980) are mixtures of cooperation and intergroup competi- tion. Team-Assisted-Instruction (Slavin, Leavey, & Madden, 1983) is a mixture of individualistic and cooperative learning. When the results of "pure" and "mixed" operationalizations of cooperative learning were compared, the "pure" operationalizations consistent- ly produced significantly higher achievement.

That working together to achieve a common goal produces higher achievement and greater productivity than does working alone is so well confirmed by so much research that it stands as one of the strongest principles of social and organizational psychol- ogy. Learning basic facts, understanding concepts, higher level reasoning, problem solving, and applying may all be best done in cooperative learning groups. The more conceptual the task, the more problem solving that is required, and the more creative the answers need to be, the greater the superiority of cooperative over competitive and individualistic learning. Cooperative learning is in- dicated whenever the learning goals are highly important, the task is complex or conceptual, problem solving is desired, divergent thinking or creativity is desired, quality of performance is expected, higher level reasoning strategies and critical thinking are needed, and long-term retention is desired.

Table 3:1

Social Interdependence: Weighted Findings

Effect-Sizes	Mean	s.d.	n
Achievement			
Cooperative Vs. Competitive	0.67	0.98	110
Cooperative Vs. Individualistic	0.67	0.84	156
Competitive vs. Individualistic	0.29	0.77	37
Interpersonal Attraction			
Cooperative Vs. Competitive	0.65	0.47	87
Cooperative Vs. Individualistic	0.64	0.59	57
Competitive vs. Individualistic	0.08	0.70	15
Social Support			
Cooperative Vs. Competitive	0.63	0.47	64
Cooperative Vs. Individualistic	0.87	0.77	65
Competitive vs. Individualistic	-0.11	0.38	18
Self-Esteem			
Cooperative Vs. Competitive	0.64	0.69	36
Cooperative Vs. Individualistic	0.46	0.34	25
Competitive vs. Individualistic	-0.19	0.36	11

Indices Of Achievement

In addition to the mastery and retention of material being studied, achievement is indicated by the quality of reasoning strategies used to complete the assignment, generating new ideas and solutions (i.e., process gain), and transferring what is learned within one situation to another (i.e., group-to-individual transfer). A number of researchers have focused on the **quality of reasoning strategy** used within competitive, individualistic, and cooperative situations. Laughlin and his colleagues (Laughlin, 1965, 1972; Laughlin & Jaccard, 1975; Laughlin, McGlynn, Anderson, & Jacobson, 1968; McGlynn, 1972) found that individuals working cooperatively used a **focusing** strategy in figuring out a concept underlying a set of numbers or words more frequently than did individuals working competitively or individualistically and, therefore, solved the problems faster. Dansereau and his colleagues (Spurlin, Dansereau, Larson, & Brooks, 1984; Larson, Dansereau, O'Donnell, Hythecker, Lambiotte, & Rocklin (1985) found that individuals in cooperative groups used elaboration and meta-cognitive strategies more frequently than did individuals working competitively and individualistically and, therefore, performed at a higher level. Numerous studies on Piaget's cognitive development theory and Kohlberg's moral development theory indicate that higher-level reasoning is promoted by cooperative experiences (see Johnson & Johnson, 1979, in press).

We and our colleagues (Gabbert, Johnson, & Johnson, 1986; D. Johnson & Johnson, 1981a; D. Johnson, Skon, & Johnson, 1980; Skon, Johnson, & Johnson, 1981) conducted a series of studies comparing student performance within competitive, individualistic, and cooperative learning situations on tasks that could be solved using either higher- or lower-level reasoning strategies. We found a more frequent discovery and use within the cooperative condition of such higher-level reasoning strategies as category search and retrieval, intersectional classification, formulating equations, sequencing, metaphoric reasoning, and conservation strategies. In the categorization and retrieval task, for example, first grade students were instructed to memorize 12 nouns during the instructional session and then to complete several retrieval tasks during the testing session the following day. The 12 nouns were given in random order and students were told to (1) order the nouns in a way that makes sense and aids memorization and (2) memorize the words. Three of the words were fruits, three were animals, three were clothing, and three were toys. Eight of the nine cooperative groups discovered and used all four categories, and only one student in the competitive and individualistic conditions did so. Salatas and Flavell (1976) found that even third-grade students had difficulty using category search procedures, yet in these studies first-grade students were able to do so after discussing the task within cooperative learning groups. Even the highest achieving students failed to use the category search strategy in the competitive and individualistic conditions (that is, cooperators benefited from collective induction).

Process gain occurs when new ideas, solutions, or efforts are generated through group interaction that are not generated when persons work individually. One of the most compelling studies of process gain was conducted by Ames and Murray (1982). They identified first- and second-grade children who were unable to understand conservation tasks. Subjects were randomly assigned to one of five conditions: (a) individualistic work, (b) being informed that a stranger had a different opinion, (c) role playing the opposite of what they had orginally answered, (d) listening to a model peer answer conservation problems, and (e) being placed in a cooperative pair with a partner who had different opinions (equally erroneous) and being required to reach consensus. Even when the two children did not know the basic principles of conservation, the cooperative condition resulted in the subjects spontaneously generating and sharing conservation judgments and explanations where none existed on the pretests. The conservation insights were sustained through both immediate and delayed posttests and affected responses to items that were not part of the experimental session. The subjects in the cooperative condition outperformed the subjects in all the other conditions on the posttests. While in the individualistic condition only 6 percent of the children gave conservation answers and explanations on the first posttest, 42 percent of the children in the cooperative condition did so.

Group-to-individual transfer occurs when individuals who learned within a cooperative group demonstrate mastery on a subsequent test taken individually. There are studies indicating that group-to-individual transfer does and does not occur after cooperative learning (Johnson & Johnson, in press). The studies that failed to find transfer of learning, however, suffered from a lack of positive interdependence, individual accountability, higher-level tasks, and discussion of the material being learned. Studies that carefully structured both positive interdependence and individual accountability within the cooperative condition, required students to discuss the material they were learning, and used higher-level tasks consistently found group-to-individual transfer.

What Mediates?

On the basis of the research conducted to date (which is considerable), it may be concluded that generally achievement is higher in cooperative situations than in competitive or individualistic ones and that cooperative efforts result in more frequent use of higher-level reasoning strategies, more frequent process gain, and higher performance on subsequent tests taken individually (group-to-individual transfer) than do competitive or individualistic efforts. These results beg the question, "Why does cooperation result in higher achievement--what mediates?"

The critical issue in understanding the relationship between cooperation and achievement is specifying the variables that mediate the relationship. Simply placing students in groups and telling them to work together does not in and of itself promote higher achievement. There are many ways in which group efforts may go wrong. Less able members sometimes "leave it to George" to complete the group's tasks thus creating a **free rider** effect (Kerr & Bruun, 1983) whereby group members expend decreasing amounts of effort and just go through the team-work motions. At the same time, the more able group member may expend less effort to avoid the **sucker effect** of doing all the work (Kerr, 1983). High ability group members may be deferred to and may take over the important leadership roles in ways that benefit them at the expense of the other group members (the **rich-get-richer** effect). In a learning group, for example, the more able group member may give all the explanations of what is being learned. Since the amount of time spent explaining correlates highly with the amount learned, the more able member learns a great deal while the less able members flounder as a captive audience. The time spent listening in group brainstorming can reduce the amount of time any individual can state their ideas (Hill, 1982; Lamm & Trommsdorff, 1973). Group efforts can be characterized by self-induced helplessness (Langer & Benevento, 1978), diffusion of responsibility and social loafing (Latane, Williams, & Harkin, 1979), ganging up against a task, reactance (Salomon, 1981), disfunctional divisions of labor ("I'm the thinkist and you're the typist") (Sheingold, Hawkins, & Char, 1984), inappropriate dependence on authority (Webb, Ender, & Lewis, 1986), destructive conflict (Collins, 1970; Johnson & Johnson, 1979), and other patterns of behavior that debilitate group performance.

It is only under certain conditions that group efforts may be expected to be more productive than individual efforts. Those conditions are:

1. Clearly perceived positive interdependence.

2. Considerable promotive (face-to-face) interaction.

3. Felt personal responsibility (individual accountability) to achieve the group's goals.

4. Frequent use of relevant interpersonal and small group skills.

5. Periodic and regular group processing.

Positive Interdependence

The first step in promoting cooperation among students is to structure positive interdependence within the learning situation. **Positive interdependence** exists when one perceives that one is linked with others in a way so that one cannot succeed unless they do (and vice versa) and/or that one must coordinate one's efforts with the efforts of others to complete a task (Johnson & Johnson, in press). Positive interdependence is the most important factor in structuring learning situations cooperatively. If students do not believe that they "sink or swim together," then the lesson is not cooperative. When students are placed in learning groups but no positive interdependence is structured, the learning situation is not cooperative, it is either competitive or individualistic with talking. Under those conditions, there is no reason to expect groups to out-perform individuals. In fact, the opposite may be true.

There are two major categories of interdependence: outcome interdependence and means interdependence (Deutsch, 1949; Thomas, 1957). How students behave in a learning situation is lar-gely determined by their perceptions of the outcomes desired and the means by which the desired goals may be reached. When per-sons are in a cooperative or competitive situation, they are oriented toward a desired **outcome**, end state, goal, or reward. If there is no outcome interdependence (goal and reward interdependence), there is no cooperation or competition. In addition, the **means** through which the mutual goals or rewards are to be accomplished specify the actions required on the part of group members. Means interdependence includes resource, role, and task interdepen-dence (which are overlapping and not independent from each other).

Positive interdependence has numerous effects on individuals' motivation and productivity, not the least of which is that it high-lights the fact that the efforts of **all** group members are needed for group success. When members of a group see their efforts as dis-pensable for the group's success, they may reduce their efforts (Kerr & Bruun, 1983; Harkins & Petty, in press; Kerr, 1983; Sweeney, 1973). When group members perceive their potential contribution to the group as being unique they increase their efforts (Harkins & Petty, 1982). When goal, task, resource, and role interdependence are clearly understood, individuals realize that their efforts are re-quired in order for the group to succeed (i.e., there can be no "free-riders') and that their contributions are often unique. In addition, reward interdependence needs to be structured to ensure that one member's efforts do not make the efforts of other members unnecessary. If the highest score in the group determined the group grade, for example, low ability members would see their efforts to produce unnecessary, they might contribute minimally, and high ability members might feel exploited and become demoralized and, therefore, decrease their efforts so as not to provide undeserved rewards for irresponsible and ungrateful "free-riders" (Kerr, 1983).

Promotive (Face-To-Face) Interaction

Promotive interaction may be defined as individuals encouraging and facilitating each other's efforts to complete tasks and achieve in order to reach the group's goals. Promotive interaction is characterized by students (a) providing other with efficient and effective help and assistance, (b) exchanging needed resources such as information and materials and processing information more efficiently and effectively, (c) providing each other with feedback in order to improve their subsequent performance on assigned tasks and responsibilities, (d) challenging each other's conclusions and reasoning in order to promote higher quality decision making and greater insight into the problems being considered, (e) advocating exerting efforts to achieve mutual goals, (f) influencing each other's efforts to achieve mutual goals, (g) acting in trusting and trustworthy ways, (h) being motivated to strive for mutual benefit, and (i) feeling less anxiety and stress (Johnson & Johnson, in press). The amount of research documenting the impact of promotive interaction on achievement is too voluminous to review here. Interested readers are referred to Johnson and Johnson (in press).

Personal Responsibility / Individual Accountability

After positive interdependence and promotive interaction, a key variable mediating the effectiveness of cooperation is a sense of **personal responsibility** to the other group members for contributing one's efforts to accomplish the group's goals. This involves being responsible for (1) completing one's share of the work and (2) facilitating the work of other group members and minimally hindering their efforts, in other words, for doing as much as one can toward achieving the group's goals. There are a number of ways in which this personal commitment/responsibility may be inculcated. The first is through structuring positive interdependence among group members so that they will feel responsible for helping each other to achieve the group's goals. The second is through the teacher assessing each individual student's level of achievement, that is, holding each individual student accountable for completing assignments and learning the assigned material.

Students are not only accountable to the teacher in cooperative situations, they are also accountable to their peers. Learning groups should be provided with information about the level of mastery of the assigned material each student is achieving. Feedback mechanisms for determining the level of each person's achievement are necessary for members to provide support and assistance to each other. When groups work on tasks where it is difficult to identify members' contributions, when there is an increased likelihood of redundant efforts, when there is a lack of group cohesiveness, and when there is lessened responsibility for the final outcome, the less some members will try to contribute to goal achievement (Harkins & Petty, 1982; Ingham, Levinger, Graves, & Peckham, 1974; Kerr & Bruun, 1981; Latane, Williams & Harkins, 1975; Moede, 1920; Petty, Harkins, Williams, & Lantane, 1977; Williams, 1981; Williams, Harkins, & Latane, 1981). If, however, there is high individual accountability and it is clear how much effort each member is contributing, if redundant efforts are avoided, if every member is responsible for the final outcome, and if the group is cohesive, then the social loafing effect vanishes. The smaller the size of the group the greater the individual accountability may be (Messich & Brewer, 1983).

Social Skills

Placing socially unskilled students in a learning group and telling them to cooperate will obviously not be successful. Students must be taught the interpersonal and small group skills needed for high quality cooperation, and be motivated to use them. And all group members must engage in them (if only the most socially skilled group members engage in all the needed leadership and communication skills, they will increase their skills at the expense of their less active and less socially skilled groupmates--the "rich-get-richer effect).

In their studies on the long-term implementation of cooperative learning, Lew and Mesch (Lew, Mesch, Johnson, & Johnson, 1986a, 1986b; Mesch, Johnson, & Johnson, 1988; Mesch, Lew, Johnson, & Johnson, 1986) investigated the impact of a reward contingency for using social skills as well as positive interdependence and a contingency for academic achievement on performance within cooperative learning groups. In the cooperative skills conditions students were trained weekly in four social skills and each member of a cooperative group was given two bonus points toward the quiz grade if all group members were observed by the teacher to demonstrate three out of four cooperative skills. The results indicated that the combination of positive interdependence, an academic contingency for high performance by all group members, and a social skills contingency, promoted the highest achievement. The more socially skillful students are, and the more attention teachers pay to teaching and rewarding the use of social skills, the higher the achievement that can be expected within cooperative learning groups.

There is only so much that structure can do. Students need to master and use interpersonal and small group skills to capitalize on the opportunities presented by a cooperative learning situation. Especially when learning groups function on a long- term basis and engage in complex, free exploratory activities over a prolonged basis, the interpersonal and small group skills of the members may determine the level of student achievement.

Group Processing

In order to achieve, students in cooperative learning groups have to work together effectively. Effective group work is influenced by whether or not groups reflect on (i.e., process) how well they are functioning. A **process** is an identifiable sequence of events taking place over time, and **process goals** refer to the sequence of events instrumental in achieving outcome goals. **Group processing** may be defined as reflecting on a group session to (a) describe what member actions were helpful and unhelpful and (b) make decisions about what actions to continue or change. The purpose of group processing is to clarify and improve the effectiveness of the members in contributing to the collaborative efforts to achieve the group's goals.

No direct evidence of the impact of group processing on achievement was available until a study was recently conducted by Stuart Yager (Yager, Johnson, & Johnson, 1985). He examined the impact on achievement of (a) cooperative learning in which members discussed how well their group was functioning and how they could improve its effectiveness, (b) cooperative learning without any group processing, and (c) individualistic learning. The results indicate that the high-, medium-, and low-achieving students in the cooperation with group processing condition achieved higher on daily achievement, post-instructional achievement, and retention measures than did the students in the other two conditions. Students in the cooperation without group processing condition, furthermore, achieved higher on all three measures than did the students in the individualistic condition.

Johnson, Johnson, Stanne, and Garibaldi (in press) conducted a follow-up study comparing cooperative learning with no processing, cooperative learning with teacher processing (teacher specified cooperative skills to use, observed, and gave whole class feedback as to how well students were using the skills), cooperative learning with teacher and student processing (teacher specified cooperative skills to use, observed, gave whole class feedback as to how well students were using the skills, and had learning groups discuss how well they interacted as a group), and individualistic learning. Forty-nine high ability Black American high school seniors and entering college freshmen at Xavier University participated in the study. A complex computer-assisted problem-solving assignment was given to all students. All three cooperative conditions performed higher than did the individualistic condition. The combination of teacher and student processing resulted in greater problem-solving success than did the other cooperative conditions.

Summary

In this section we addressed two key questions about the relationship between cooperation and achievement:

1. What is the relative impact on achievement of competitive, individualistic, and cooperative efforts?

2. What are the variables mediating or moderating the relationship between cooperation and achievement?

Over 323 studies have been conducted over the past 90 years comparing the relative impact of cooperative, competitive, and individualistic learning situations on achievement. On the basis of this research, it may be concluded that generally achievement is higher in cooperative situations than in competitive or individualistic ones and that cooperative efforts result in more frequent use of higher-level reasoning strategies, more frequent process gain and collective induction, and higher performance on subsequent tests taken individually (group-to-individual transfer) than do competitive or individualistic efforts.

The critical issue in understanding the relationship between cooperation and achievement is specifying the variables that mediate the relationship. Simply placing students in groups and telling them to work together does not in and of itself promote higher achievement. There are many ways in which group efforts may go wrong. It is only under certain conditions that group efforts may be expected to be more productive than individual efforts. There is evidence that cooperative learning will only be effective when teachers structure and promote:

1. Clearly perceived positive interdependence.

2. Considerable promotive (face-to-face) interaction.

3. Felt personal responsibility (individual accountability) to achieve the group's goals.

4. Frequent use of relevant interpersonal and small group skills.

5. Periodic and regular group processing.

Currently students believe that a learning task is completed when they have an answer in every blank in a worksheet. Sustained effort to comprehend material deeply seems to be rare. The Japanese, on the other hand, view academic success as a matter of disciplined, enduring effort aimed at achieving **satori**, or the sudden flash of enlightenment that comes after long, intensive, but successful effort. The achievement of satori is much more likely after a discussion in cooperative learning groups than after working alone, competitively, or individualistically to complete an assignment.

Other Outcomes

Critical Thinking Competencies

In many subject areas related to science and technology the teaching of facts and theories is considered to be secondary to the teaching of critical thinking and the use of higher level reasoning strategies. The aim of science education, for example, has been to develop individuals "who can sort sense from nonsense," or who have the critical thinking abilities of grasping information, examining it, evaluating it for soundness, and applying it appropriately. Cooperative learning promotes a greater use of higher reasoning strategies and critical thinking than do competitive and individualistic learning strategies (Johnson & Johnson, 1983, in press).

Interpersonal Relationships

Cooperative learning experiences, compared with competitive, individualistic, and "traditional instruction," promote considerably more liking among students (Johnson & Johnson, 1983, in press; Johnson, Johnson, & Maruyama, 1983). This is true regardless of differences in ability level, sex, handicapping conditions, ethnic membership, social class differences, or task orientation. Students who collaborate on their studies develop considerable commitment and caring for each other no matter what their initial impressions of and attitudes toward each other were. We have conducted a series of studies on mainstreaming, ethnic integration, and relationships between males and females to determine whether there are limits to the impact of cooperation on liking among students. So far none have been found.

In addition to our own research we recently completed a meta-analysis of all existing research on the relative impact of cooperative, competitive, and individualistic learning experiences on interpersonal attraction among homogeneous and heterogeneous samples of students (Johnson & Johnson, in-press; Johnson, Johnson, & Maruyama, 1983). Cooperation (compared with competitive and individualistic efforts) results in more positive interpersonal relations among individuals (regardless of differences in ability (effect sizes of ethnic background, handicaps, or sex) (effect sizes of 0.65 and 0.64 respectively). In order to be productive, a class of students (or a school faculty) has to cohere and have a positive emotional climate. As relationships become more positive, absenteeism decreases, and increases may be expected in student commitment to learning, feelings of personal responsibility to do the assigned work, willingness to take on difficult tasks, motivation and persistence in working on learning tasks, satisfaction and morale, willingness to endure pain and frustration to succeed, willingness to defend the school against external criticism or attack, willingness to listen to and be influenced by peers, commitment to peer's success and growth, and productivity and achievement (Johnson & F. Johnson, 1987; Watson & Johnson, 1972). In addition, within classrooms in which students are heterogeneous with regard to ethnic, social class, language, and ability differences, cooperative learning experiences are a necessity for building positive peer relationships.

Attitudes Toward Subject Area

Our research indicates that cooperative learning experiences, compared with competitive and individualistic ones, promote more positive attitudes toward both the subject area and the instructional experience, as well as more continuing motivation to learn more about the subject area being studied (Johnson & Johnson, 1983, in press).

Social Skills

Schooling is future-oriented in the sense that the instruction taking place is primarily aimed at preparing students for career and adult responsibilities. And the assumption is made that students will be able to apply successfully what they learn in school to career, family, community, and society settings. The industrial strategy of Japan is a good illustration of this principle. Japanese management has been quoted as stating that the superiority of the Japanese industrial system is not based on the fact that their workers are more intelligent than are the workers of other countries, but that their workers are better able to work in harmony and cooperation with each other, a goal that major U.S. companies have been working toward for years. Our research shows that there is considerable evidence that students working together in cooperative learning groups master social skills at a higher level than do students studying competitively or individualistically (Johnson & Johnson, 1983, in press).

Psychological Health

When students leave school, we would hope that they would have the psychological health and stability required to build and maintain career, family, and community relationships, to establish a basic and meaningful interdependence with other people, and to participate effectively in our society. Our studies (Johnson & Johnson, 1983, in press) indicate that **cooperativeness** is positively related to a number of indices of psychological health, namely: emotional maturity, well-adjusted social relations, strong personal identity, and basic trust in and optimism about people. **Competitiveness** seems also to be related to a number of indices of psychological health, while **individualistic attitudes** tend to be related to a number of indices of psychological pathology, emotional immaturity, social maladjustment, delinquency, self-alienation, and self-rejection. To the degree that schools can contribute to a student's psychological well-being, they should be organized to reinforce those traits and tendencies that promote it.

Accuracy of Perspective Taking

Social perspective taking is the ability to understand how a situation appears to another person and how that person is reacting cognitively and emotionally to the situation. The opposite of perspective taking is **egocentrism**, the embeddedness in one's own viewpoint to the extent that one is unaware of other points of view and of the limitations of one's perspectives. Cooperative learning experiences tend to promote greater cognitive and affective perspective taking than do competitive or individualistic learning experiences (Johnson & Johnson, 1983, in press).

Differentiation of Views of Others

Stereotypes usually focus on only a few characteristics of a person and remain static (remaining unchanged from situation to situation). Views of other students alternatively may become differentiated (taking into account many different characteristics), dynamic (being modified from situation to situation), and realistic. Cooperative learning experiences tend to promote more differentiated, dynamic, and realistic views (and therefore less stereotypes and static views) of other students (including handicapped peers and students from different ethnic groups) than do competitive and individualistic learning experiences (Johnson & Johnson, 1983, in press).

Self-Esteem

The data in Table 3.1 indicate that cooperation produced higher levels of self-esteem than did competitive and individualistic efforts (effect-sizes of 0.64 and 0.46 respectively). Individuals with low self-esteem tend to (Johnson & Johnson, in press):

1. Have low productivity due to setting low goals for themselves, lacking confidence in their ability, and assuming that they will fail no matter how hard they try.

2. Be critical of others as well as themselves by looking for flaws in others and trying to "tear them down."

3. Withdraw socially due to feeling awkward, self-conscious, and vulnerable to rejection.

4. Be conforming, agreeable, highly persuasible, and highly influenced by criticism.

5. Develop more psychological problems such as anxiety, nervousness, insomnia, depression, and psychosomatic symptoms.

Within competitive situations self-esteem tends to be based on the contingent view of one's competence that, "If I win, then I have worth as a person, but if I lose, then I have no worth." Within competitive situations winners attribute their success to superior ability and attribute the failure of others to lack of ability. Self-aggrandizement results. Only a few individuals win. The vast majority lose. Defensiveness results, which often takes the form of self-disparagement, evaluation apprehension, and the psychological and physical withdrawal from the situation. Within individualistic situations, individuals are isolated from one another and receive no direct comparison or feedback as to others' perceptions of their competence. Whatever evaluations others make of their competence are often perceived to be inaccurate and unrealistic. A defensive avoidance, evaluation apprehension, and distrust of peers results. Within cooperative situations, individuals tend to interact, promote each other's success, form multi-dimensional and realistic impressions of each other's competencies, and give accurate feedback. Such interaction tends to promote a basic self-acceptance of oneself as a competent person.

Expectations Toward Future Interaction

Cooperative learning experiences tend to promote expectations toward more rewarding and enjoyable future interaction among students (Johnson & Johnson, 1983, in press).

Relationships with School Personnel

Cooperative learning experiences not only affect relationships with other students, they also affect relationships with adults in the school. Students participating in cooperative learning experiences, compared with students participating in competitive and individualistic learning experiences, like the teacher better and perceive the teacher as being more supportive and accepting academically and personally (Johnson & Johnson, 1983, in press).

What About School Staff?

Teacher effectiveness is closely related to cooperative efforts. For teachers to improve their instructional effectiveness, they must continually improve their teaching expertise. Teaching expertise begins with mastering teaching strategies conceptually. Teachers must conceptually understand (a) the nature of the strategies they are using, (b) how to implement the strategies step-by-step, and (c) the results expected from the effective implementation of the strategies. Teachers must also think critically about the strategy and adapt it to their specific students and subject areas. They must retain what they have learned, integrate it into their conceptual networks about teaching, and conceptually combine the new strategy with their existing teaching strategies. Such conceptual understanding is enhanced when teachers **orally summarize, explain, and elaborate** what they know about the teaching strategy to colleagues. Oral reviews consolidate and strengthen what is known and provide relevant feedback about the degree to which mastery and understanding have been achieved. The way people conceptualize material and organize it cognitively is markedly different when they are learning material for their own benefit and when they are learning material to teach to others (Murray, 1983). Material being learned to be taught is learned at a higher conceptual level than is material being learned for one's own use. Such discussions, furthermore, enable the listeners to benefit from others' knowledge, reasoning, and skills. The concept of "gatekeeper," for example, was created to explain the process of information flow through an organization. A **gatekeeper** is a colleague who is sought out to explain what a new strategy is and how it may be used.

Once a strategy has been conceptually mastered, it must be implemented. If teachers are to progress through the initial awkward and mechanical stages to a routine-use, automatic level of mastery, they must (a) receive continual feedback as to the accuracy of their implementation and (b) be encouraged to persevere in their implementation attempts long enough to integrate the new strategy into their ongoing instructional practice. Thus, productivity hinges on having colleagues to coplan and coteach lessons, observe one's implementation efforts, provide feedback, and encourage one to keep trying until the strategy is used routinely without conscious thought. Needless to say, such procedural learning usually does not take place within competitive and individualistic situations.

Reducing The Discrepancy

With the amount of research evidence available, it is surprising that classroom practice is so oriented toward individualistic and competitive learning and schools are so dominated by a competitive / individualistic structure. **It is time for the discrepancy to be reduced between what research indicates is effective in teaching and what teachers actually do.** In order to do so, educators must understand the basic elements of structuring situations cooperatively, the variety of ways cooperative learning may be used in the classroom, and the role of the teacher in implementing formal cooperative learning experiences. The use of cooperative learning is the focus of the next chapter.

It is also time for the discrepancy to be reduced between what research indicates is effective in staff relations and how teachers are organized to achieve the school's goals. The ways cooperation may be used to promote the effectiveness of teachers and schools are covered in Chapters 5, 6, 7, 8, and 9.

Chapter 4

Cooperative Learning

Empowering Students Through Cooperative Learning

The most important of all the five leadership practices is empowering individuals by organizing them into cooperative teams. Such empowerment begins in the classroom. Students often feel helpless and discouraged. Giving them cooperative learning partners provides hope and opportunity. Cooperative learning groups empower their members to act by making them feel strong, capable, and committed. It is social support from and accountability to valued peers that motivates committed efforts to achieve and succeed. If classrooms are to be places where students care about each other and are committed to each other's success in academic endeavors, a cooperative structure must exist. To understand how to empower students through cooperative learning groups you must understand the types of social interdependence, the five basic elements of good cooperative learning, and the types of cooperative learning that may be used in the classroom.

Types Of Social Interdependence

An essential instructional skill that all teachers need is knowing how and when to structure students' learning goals competitively, individualistically, and cooperatively. By structuring positive, negative, or no interdependence, teachers can influence the pattern of interaction among students and the instructional outcomes that result (Deutsch, 1962; Johnson & Johnson, 1987a, 1988; Johnson, Johnson, & Holubec, 1986).

Each time teachers prepare for a lesson, they must make decisions about the teaching strategies they will use. Teachers may structure academic lessons so that students are (a) in a win-lose struggle to see who is best, (b) learning individually on their own without interacting with classmates, or (c) learning in pairs or small groups helping each other master the assigned material. When lessons are structured competitively, students work against each other to achieve a goal that only one or a few students can attain. Students are graded on a curve, which requires them to work faster and more accurately than their peers. In a **competitive** learning situation, students' goal achievements are negatively correlated; when one student achieves his or her goal, all others with whom he or she is competitively linked fail to achieve their goals. Students seek outcomes that are personally beneficial but also are detrimental to the others with whom they are competitively linked. They either study hard to do better than their classmates or they take it easy because they do not believe they have a chance to win. In a competitively structured class, students would be given the task of completing the assignments faster and more accurately than the other students in the class. They would be warned to work by themselves, without discussing the assignments with other students, and to seek help from the teacher if they needed it.

Teachers can structure lessons individualistically so that students work by themselves to accomplish learning goals unrelated to those of their classmates. Individual goals are assigned each day, students' efforts are evaluated on a fixed set of standards, and rewards are given accordingly. Each student has a set of materials and works at his or her own speed, ignoring the other students in the class. In an **individualistic** learning situation, students' goal achievements are independent; the goal achievement of one student is unrelated to the goal achievement of others. Students seek outcomes that are personally beneficial and they ignore as irrelevant the goal achievements of their classmates. In a class structured individualistically, students would be given the task of completing the assignments correctly to reach a preset criterion of excellence. Students would be told to work by themselves, without disturbing their neighbors, and to seek help and assistance from the teacher.

For the past 45 years competitive and individualistic goal structures have dominated American education. Students usually come to school with competitive expectations and pressures from their parents. Many teachers have tried to reduce classroom competition by switching from a norm-referenced to a criteria-referenced evaluation system. In both competitive and individualistic learning situations teachers try to keep students away from each other. "Do not copy!" "Move your desks apart!" "I want to see how well you can do, not your neighbor!" are all phrases that teachers commonly use in their classrooms. Students are repeatedly told, "Do not care about the other students in this class. Take care of yourself!" When a classroom is dominated by competition, students often experience classroom life as a "rat race" with the psychology of the 100-yard dash. When a classroom is dominated by individualistic efforts, students will concentrate on isolating themselves from each other, ignoring others, and focusing only on their own work. Many students begin to compete within individualistic situations, even though the structure does not require it.

There is a third option. Teachers can structure lessons cooperatively so that students work together to accomplish shared goals. Students are assigned to small groups and instructed to learn the assigned material and to make sure that the other members of the group also master the assignment. Individual performance is checked regularly to ensure all students are learning. A criteria-referenced evaluation system is used. In a **cooperative** learning situation, students' goal achievements are positively correlated; students perceive that they can reach their learning goals if and only if the other students in the learning group also reach their goals. Thus, students seek outcomes that are beneficial to all those with whom they are cooperatively linked. Students discuss material with each other, help one another understand it, and encourage each other to work hard. In a cooperatively structured class, heterogeneous small groups made up of one high, one medium, and one low ability student would be formed. The students are given three tasks: to learn the assigned material, to make sure that the other members of their group have learned the assigned material, and to make sure that everyone in the class has learned the assigned material. While the students work on assignments, they discuss the the material with the other members of their group, explaining how to complete the work, listening to each other's explanations, encouraging each other to try to understand the solutions, and providing academic help and assistance. When everyone in the group has mastered the material, they go look for another group to help until everyone in the class understands how to complete the assignments.

Cooperative learning is the most important of the three ways of structuring learning situations, yet it is currently the least used. In most schools, class sessions are structured cooperatively only for 7 to 20 percent of the time (Johnson & Johnson, 1983a). The research indicates, however, that cooperative learning should be used whenever teachers want students to learn more, like school better, like each other better, have higher self-esteem, and learn more effective social skills.

Basic Elements Of Cooperative Learning

Many teachers believe that they are implementing cooperative learning when in fact they are missing its essence. Putting students into groups to learn is not the same thing as structuring cooperation among students. Cooperation is **not**:

1. Having students sit side by side at the same table and talk with each other as they do their individual assignments.

2. Having students do a task individually with instructions that the ones who finish first are to help the slower students.

3. Assigning a report to a group where one student does all the work and others put their name on it.

Cooperation is much more than being physically near other students, discussing material with other students, helping other students, or sharing materials with other students, although each of these is important in cooperative learning.

In order for a lesson to be cooperative, five basic elements are essential and need to be included (Johnson & Johnson, 1987a; Johnson, Johnson, & Holubec, 1986, 1987, 1988). In a math class, for example, a teacher assigns her students a set of math story problems to solve. Students are placed in groups of three. The **instructional task** is for the students to solve each story problem correctly and understand the correct strategy for doing so. The teacher must now implement the five basic elements. The first element of a cooperative lesson to be included is **positive interdependence**. Students must believe that they are linked with others in a way that one cannot succeed unless the other members of the group succeed (and vice versa). In other words, students must perceive that they "sink or swim together." Within the math story problems lesson, positive interdependence is structured by group members (1) agreeing on the answer and the strategies for solving each problem (goal interdependence) and (2) fulfilling assigned role responsibilities (role interdependence). Each group is given a set of story problems (one copy for each student) and a set of three "role" cards. Each group member is assigned one of the roles. The **reader** reads the problems aloud to the group. The **checker** makes sure that all members can explain how to solve each problem correctly. The **encourager** in a friendly way encourages all members of the group to participate in the discussion, sharing their ideas and feelings. Other ways of structuring positive interdependence includes having common rewards, being dependent on each other's resources, or a division of labor.

The second element of a cooperative lesson is **face-to-face promotive interaction** among students. This exists when students orally explain to each other how to solve problems, discuss with each other the nature of the concepts and strategies being learned, teach one's knowledge to classmates, and explain to each other the connections between present and past learning. This face-to-face interaction is **promotive** in the sense that students help, assist, encourage, and support each other's efforts to learn. In the math lesson, the teacher must provide the time and encouragement for students to exchange ideas and help each other learn.

The third element is **individual accountability**. The teacher needs to ensure that the performance of each individual student is assessed and the results given back to the group and the individual. It is important that the group knows who needs more assistance in completing the assignment and it is important that group members know they cannot "hitch-hike" on the work of others. Common ways to structure individual accountability include giving an individual test to each student and randomly selecting one student's work to represent the entire group. In the math lesson, since group members certify that all members (1) have the correct answer written on their answer sheets and (2) can correctly explain how to solve each problem, individual accountability is structured by having the teacher pick one answer sheet at random to score for the group and randomly asking one group member to explain how to solve one of the problems.

The fourth element is **social skills**. Groups cannot function effectively if students do not have and use the needed leadership, decision-making, trust-building, communication, and conflict-management skills. These skills have to be taught just as purposefully and precisely as academic skills. Many students have never worked cooperatively in learning situations and, therefore, lack the needed social skills for doing so. Today, the math teacher is emphasizing the skill of "making sure everyone understands." When the teacher sees students engaging in the skill, she verbally praises the group and puts a star on the group's paper. Procedures and strategies for teaching students social skills may be found in Johnson (1986, 1987), Johnson and F. Johnson (1987), and Johnson, Johnson, and Holubec (1986, 1988a).

Finally, the teacher must ensure that **groups process** how well they are achieving their goals and maintaining effective working relationships among members. At the end of the math period the groups process their functioning by answering two questions: (1) What is something each member did that was helpful for the group and (2) What is something each member could do to make the group even better tomorrow? Such processing enables learning groups to focus on group maintenance, facilitates the learning of collaborative skills, ensures that members receive feedback on their participation, and reminds students to practice collaborative skills consistently. Some of the keys to successful processing are allowing sufficient time for it to take place, making it specific rather than vague, maintaining student involvement in processing, reminding students to use their collaborative skills while they process, and ensuring that clear expectations of the purpose of processing have been communicated (Johnson & Johnson, 1985, 1987a; Johnson, Johnson, & Holubec, 1986, 1988a).

Types Of Cooperative Learning

"The best answer to the question, 'What is the most effective method of teaching?' is that it depends on the goal, the student, the content, and the teacher. But the next best answer is, 'Students teaching other students.' There is a wealth of evidence that peer teaching is extremely effective for a wide range of goals, content, and students of different levels and personalities."

Wilbert McKeachie, et al. (1986, p. 63).

In order to maximize their achievement, especially when studying conceptually complex and content-dense material, students should not be allowed to be passive while they are learning. One way to get students more actively involved in this process is to structure cooperative interaction into classes so that students have to explain what they are learning to each other, learn each other's point of view, give and receive support from classmates, and help each other dig below the superficial level of understanding of the material they are learning. It is vital for students to have peer support and to be active learners, not only so that more students learn the material, but so that they get to know other students in class and build a sense of community that centers on the academic side of the school. It is equally important that when seniors graduate they have developed skills in talking through material with peers, listening with real skill, knowing how to build trust in a working relationship, and providing leadership to group efforts. Without developing and practicing the social skills required to work cooperatively with others, how can faculty honestly claim that they have prepared students for a world where they will need to coordinate their efforts with others on the job, skillfully keep a marriage and family functioning, and be a contributing member of a community and society? Getting students actively engaged with each other, working cooperatively in the classroom, is critical for the reasons outlined and many more.

Cooperative learning may be incorporated into courses through the use of: **formal learning groups,** which are more structured and stay together until the task is done; **informal learning groups,** which are short-term and less structured; and **base groups,** which are long-term groups whose role is primarily one of peer support and long-term accountability.

Formal Cooperative Learning Groups

Formal cooperative learning groups may last for several minutes to several class sessions to complete a specific task or assignment (such as solving a set of problems, completing a unit, writing a report or theme, conducting an experiment, and reading and comprehending a story, play, chapter, or book). It is within formal cooperative learning groups that jigsawing course material, group problem-solving and decision-making assignments, laboratory projects, simulations, writing/peer-editing assignments, experiential exercises, and class presentations are all used. **Any course requirement or assignment may be reformulated to be cooperative rather than competitive or individualistic through the use of formal cooperative learning groups.** Mastering how to structure and conduct lessons that include formal cooperative learning groups is the first step in becoming competent in using cooperative learning procedures. **Gaining expertise in using formal cooperative learning groups provides the foundation for gaining expertise in using informal and base groups.**

When using formal cooperative learning groups, the teacher is both an academic expert **and** a classroom manager to promote effective group functioning. The teacher structures the learning groups; teaches the academic concepts, principles, and strategies that the students are to master and apply; and then monitors the functioning of the learning groups and intervenes to (a) teach collaborative skills and (b) provide assistance in academic learning when it is needed. Students are taught to look to their peers for assistance, feedback, reinforcement, and support. Students are expected to interact with each other, share ideas and materials, support and encourage academic achievement, orally explain and elaborate the concepts and strategies being learned, and hold each other accountable for learning. A criteria-referenced evaluation system is used.

Implementing cooperative learning involves a structured, but complex, process. Teachers are encouraged to start small by taking one class and using cooperative learning procedures until the process feels comfortable to them and then expanding into other classes. When structuring lessons cooperatively, teachers must complete the following five sets of activities (Johnson & Johnson, 1984, 1987a; Johnson, Johnson, & Holubec, 1987):

1. Clearly specify the objectives for the lesson.

2. Make a number of decisions about placing students in learning groups before the lesson is taught.

3. Clearly explain the task, the positive interdependence, and the learning activity to the students.

4. Monitor the effectiveness of cooperative learning groups and intervene to provide task assistance (such as answering questions and teaching task skills) or to increase students' interpersonal and group skills.

5. Evaluate the students' achievement and help students discuss how well they collaborated with each other.

The following discussion elaborates on these activities and details a procedure for structuring cooperative learning. Specific examples of lessons may be found in Johnson, Johnson, & Holubec, (1987). Two films are also available that demonstrate the use of cooperative learning procedures (**Belonging, Circles Of Learning**). More complete descriptions of how to structure cooperative learning may be found in **Cooperation In The Classroom** (Johnson, Johnson, & Holubec, 1988), **Learning Together And Alone: Cooperative, Competitive, And Individualistic Learning** (Johnson & Johnson, 1987a), and **Circles Of Learning, Revised Edition** (Johnson, Johnson, & Holubec, 1986).

Objectives

Two types of objectives need to be specified before the lesson begins: (1) an academic objective specified at the correct level for the students and matched to the right level of instruction, and (2) a collaborative skills objective detailing what interpersonal and small group skills are going to be emphasized during the lesson. A common error many teachers make is to specify only academic objectives and to ignore the collaborative skills objectives needed to train students to cooperate with each other.

Decisions

Deciding On the Size Of Group. Cooperative learning groups tend to range in size from two to six. When students are inexperienced in working cooperatively, when time is short, and when materials are scarce, the size of the group should be two to three. When students become more experienced and skillful, they will be able to manage groups of four or five members. Cooperative learning groups need to be small enough so that every student has to participate actively. A common mistake is to have students work in groups of four, five, and six before the students have the skills to do so competently.

Assigning Students To Groups. Teachers may wish to assign students to ability heterogeneous learning groups. When working on a specific skill, procedure, or set of facts, homogeneous groups may be useful. When working on problem-solving tasks and on learning basic concepts heterogeneous groups may be most appropriate. When in doubt, teachers should use heterogeneous groups where students of different achievement levels in math, ethnic backgrounds, sexes, and social classes work together. Teachers will want to take special care in building a group where students who have special learning problems in math or who are isolated from their peers will be accepted and encouraged to achieve. At other times random assignment of students to groups is often effective.

Planning How Long Groups Will Work Together. The third decision teachers make is how long to keep groups together. Some teachers assign students to groups that last a whole semester or even a whole academic year. Other teachers like to keep a learning group together only long enough to complete a unit or chapter. In some schools student attendance is so unpredictable that teachers form new groups each day. Sooner or later, however, every math student should work with every other classmate. Usually it is preferable to keep groups together for at least two or three weeks.

Arranging The Room. Members of a learning group should sit close enough to each other that they can share materials and talk to each other quietly and maintain eye contact with all group members. Circles are usually best. The teacher should have clear access lanes to every group. Common mistakes that teachers make in arranging a room are to (1) place students at a rectangular table where they cannot have eye contact with all other members or (2) move desks together, which may place students too far apart to communicate quietly with each other and share materials.

Planning Materials. Instructional materials need to be distributed among group members so that all students participate and achieve. Especially when students are inexperienced in cooperating, teachers will want to distribute materials in ways planned to communicate that the assignment is a joint (not an individual) effort and that students are in a "sink or swim together" learning situation. One way is to give only one copy of the materials to a group to ensure thtat the students will have to work together. Materials can be arranged like a jigsaw puzzle so that each student has part of the materials needed to complete the task. The steps for structuring a jigsaw lesson are to (1) distribute a set of materials to each group, divide the materials into parts, and give each member one part; (2) assign students the individual tasks of learning and becoming an expert on their part of the material and planning how to teach the material to the other group members; (3) have each student meet with a member of another learning group who is learning the same section of the materials and conferring about how to best teach the section to other group members (expert pairs); and (4) have the groups meet and the members teach their area of expertise to the other group members so that all students learn all the assigned material.

Assigning Roles. Cooperative interdependence may also be arranged through the assignment of complementary and interconnected roles to group members. Such roles might include a **summarizer** (who restates the group's major conclusions or answers), a **checker** (who makes sure that all members can explain how to arrive at an answer or conclusion), an **accuracy coach** (who corrects any mistakes in another member's explanations or summaries), and a **relater** (who asks other members to relate current concepts and strategies to material studied previously). Assigning students such roles is an effective method of teaching them cooperative skills and fostering interdependence.

Explaining The Academic Task And Cooperative Goal Structure

Explaining The Academic Task. Teachers explain the academic task so that students are clear about the assignment and understand the objectives of the lesson. Direct teaching of concepts, principles, and strategies may take place at this point. Teachers may wish to answer any questions students have about the concepts or facts they are to learn or apply in the lesson.

Structuring Positive Goal Interdependence. Teachers communicate to students that they have a group goal and must work collaboratively. This may be done by asking the group to produce a single product or report, arrive at consensus concerning how assigned problems are solved, providing group rewards, giving bonus points if all members of a group reach a preset criteria of excellence, or picking a student at random to represent the group and explain its conclusions to the class. In a cooperative learning group, students are responsible for learning the assigned material, making sure that all other group members learn the assigned material, and making sure that all other class members learn the assigned material, in that order.

Structuring Individual Accountability. The purpose of the learning group is to maximize the learning of each member. Lessons need to be structured so that the level of each student's learning is assessed and that groups provide members with the encouragement and assistance needed to maximize individual performance. Individual accountability may be structured by having each student individually tested or randomly choosing the work of one member to represent the group as a whole.

Structuring Intergroup Cooperation. The positive outcomes found with a cooperative learning group can be extended throughout a whole class by structuring intergroup cooperation. Bonus points or other rewards may be given if all members of a class reach a preset criteria of excellence. When a group finishes its work, the teacher should encourage the members to go help other groups complete the assignment, and learn the material.

Explaining Criteria For Success. Evaluations within cooperatively structured lessons need to be criteria-referenced. At the beginning of the lesson teachers need to explain clearly the criteria by which students' work will be evaluated.

Specifying Desired Behaviors. The word cooperative has many different connotations and uses. Teachers will need to define cooperation operationally by specifying the behaviors that are appropriate and desirable within the learning groups. Beginning behaviors are "stay with your group," "use quiet voices," and "take turns." When groups begin to function effectively, expected behaviors may include "each member explains how to get an answer" and "each member relates what is being learned to previous learning."

Monitoring And Intervening

Monitoring Students' Behavior. The teacher's job begins in earnest when the cooperative learning groups begin working. Much of the teacher's time is spent observing group members to see what skillful actions they can note and praise and what problems members have completing the assignment and working coopera- tively. Many teachers also use student observers to gather infor- mation on the appropriateness of activities within each group.

Providing Academic Assistance. In monitoring the learning groups as they work, teachers will wish to clarify instructions, review important concepts and strategies, answer questions, and teach academic skills as necessary.

Intervening To Teach Cooperative Skills. While monitoring the learning groups, teachers often find students who do not have the necessary cooperative skills and groups where members are having problems in collaborating. In these cases, the teacher should intervene to suggest more effective procedures for working together and more effective behaviors in which students should engage. Basic interpersonal and small group skills may be direct- ly taught (Johnson, 1986, 1987; Johnson & F. Johnson, 1987).

Providing Closure To Lesson. At the end of each lesson, stu- dents should be able to summarize what they have learned. Teachers may wish to summarize the major points in the lesson, ask students to recall ideas or give examples, and answer any final questions students have.

Evaluation And Processing

Evaluating Students' Learning. Students' work is evaluated, their learning assessed, and feedback is given as to how their work compares with the criteria of excellence. Quality as well as quan- tity should be addressed.

Assessing How Well The Group Functioned. The learning groups assess how well they worked together and plan how to improve their effectiveness in the future. Our two favorite questions for doing so are: "What actions helped the group work productively? What actions could be added to make the group even more productive tomorrow?" When processing is taken seriously, the quality of the group interactions improve dramatically, which in turn improves achievement. A common error of many teachers is to provide too brief a time for students to process the quality of their collaboration.

Structuring Academic Controversies

Within cooperative groups students often disagree as to what answers to assignments should be and how the group should function in order to maximize members' learning. Conflict is an inherent part of learning as old conclusions and conceptions are challenged and modified to take into account new information and broader perspectives. **Controversy** is a type of academic conflict that exists when one student's ideas, information, conclusions, theories, and opinions are incompatible with those of another, and the two seek to reach an agreement. When students become experienced in working cooperatively, and when teachers wish to increase students' emotional involvement in learning and motivation to achieve, teachers may structure controversy into cooperative learning groups by structuring five phases (Johnson & Johnson, 1987b; Johnson, Johnson, & Smith, 1986):

1. Assign students to groups of four, then divide the group into two pairs. One pair is given the pro position and the other pair is given the con position on an issue being studied. Each pair prepares their position.

2. Each pair presents its position to the other pair.

3. Students argue the two positions.

4. Pairs reverse perspectives and argue the opposing position.

5. Groups of four reach a decision and come to a consensus on a position that is supported by facts and logic and can be defended by each group member.

Teacher's Role Summary

Implementing cooperative learning is not easy. It can take years to become an expert. Teachers may wish to start small by taking one subject area or one class and using cooperative learning procedures until they feel comfortable teaching cooperatively, and then expand into other subject areas or other classes. In order to implement cooperative learning successfully, teachers will need to organize themselves into colleagial support groups to promote their own and colleagues' competence and make cooperation a way of life within their classrooms and schools.

Informal Cooperative Learning Groups

Informal cooperative learning groups are temporary, ad hoc groups that last for only one discussion or one class period. Their **purposes** are to focus student attention on the material to be learned, set a mood conducive to learning, help organize in advance the material to be covered in a class session, ensure that students cognitively process the material being taught, and provide closure to an instructional session. They may be used at any time, but are especially useful during a lecture or direct teaching before the students' eyes begin to glaze over (some estimates of the length of time that people can attend to a lecture is around 12 to 15 minutes; students then need to process what they are hearing or their minds drift away). During direct teaching the instructional challenge for the teacher is to ensure that students do the intellectual work of organizing material, explaining it, summarizing it, and integrating it into existing conceptual networks. This may be achieved by having students do the advance organizing, cognitively process what they are learning, and provide closure to the lesson. Breaking up lectures with short cooperative processing times will give you slightly less lecture time, but will enhance what is learned and build relationships among the students in your class. It will help counter what is proclaimed as the main problem of lectures: "The information passes from the notes of the professor to the notes of the student without passing through the mind of either one."

The following procedure may help to plan a lecture that keeps students actively engaged intellectually. It entails having **focused discussions** before and after a lecture (i.e., bookends) and interspersing **turn-to-your-partner** discussions throughout the lecture.

1. **Focused Discussion 1**: Plan your lecture around a series of questions that the lecture answers. Prepare the questions on an overhead transparency or write them on the board so that students can see them. Have students discuss the questions in pairs. The discussion task is aimed at promoting **advance organizing** of what the students know about the topic to be presented and **set expectations** about what the lecture will cover.

2. **Turn-To-Your-Partner Discussions**: Divide the lecture into 10 to 15 minute segments. This is about the length of time an adult can concentrate on a lecture. Plan a short discussion task to be given to pairs of students after each segment. The task needs to be short enough that students can complete it within three or four minutes. Its purpose is to ensure that students are actively thinking about the material being presented. The discussion task may be to:

   a. Summarize the answer to the question being discussed.

b. Give a reaction to the theory, concepts, or information being presented.

c. Elaborate (relate material to past learning so that it gets integrated into existing conceptual frameworks) the material being presented.

d. Predict what is going to be presented next.

e. Attempt to resolve the conceptual conflict the presentation has aroused.

f. Hypothesize answers to the question being posed.

Each discussion task should have four components: **formulate** an answer to the question being asked, **share** your answer with your partner, **listen** carefully to his or her answer, and **create** a new answer that is superior to each member's initial formulation through the processes of association, building on each other's thoughts, and synthesizing. Students will need to gain some experience with this procedure to become skilled in doing it within a short period of time.

3. **Focused Discussion 2:** Prepare an ending discussion task to summarize what students have learned from the lecture. The discussion should result in students integrating what they have just learned into existing conceptual frameworks. The task may also point students toward what the homework will cover or what will be presented in the next class session. This provides closure to the lecture.

Once such preparation is completed the lecture may be given by:

1. Having students choose partners. The person nearest them will do. You may wish to require different seating arrange-

ments each class period so that students will meet and interact with a number of other students in the class.

2. Giving the pairs the cooperative assignment of completing the initial (advance organizer) task. Give them only four or five minutes to do so.

3. Delivering the first segment of the lecture. Then give the pairs a discussion task. Give them only three or four minutes to complete it. Use the **formulate/share/listen/create** procedure. Randomly choose two or three students to give 30 second summaries of their discussions.

   It is important that students are randomly called on to share their answers after each discussion task. Such **individual accountability** ensures that the pairs take the tasks seriously and check each other to ensure that both are prepared to answer.

4. Delivering the second segment of the lecture and then give a second discussion task. Repeat this sequence until the lecture is completed.

5. Giving students the ending focused discussion task to provide closure to the lecture. Give students five or six minutes to summarize and discuss the material covered in the lecture.

6. Processing the procedure with students regularly to help them increase their skill and speed in completing short discussion tasks. Processing questions may include (a) how well prepared were you to complete the discussion tasks and (b) how could you come even better prepared tomorrow?

The informal cooperative learning group is not only effective for getting students actively involved in understanding what they are learning, it also provides time for you to gather your wits, reorganize your notes, take a deep breath, and move around the class listening to what students are saying. Listening to student discussions can give you direction and insight into how the concepts you are teaching are being grasped by your students (who, unfortunately, do not have graduate degrees in the topic you are presenting).

Enemies of the Lecture

Whenever you give a lecture, you are faced with a number of enemies:

1. **Students who are preoccupied with what happened during the previous hour or with what happened on the way to class.** In order for lectures to succeed you must focus student attention on the subject area and topic you are dealing with in class.

2. **Emotional moods that block learning and cognitive processing of information.** Students who are angry or frustrated about something are **not** open to new learning. In order for lectures to work, you must set a constructive learning mood.

3. **Students who go to sleep or who turn on a tape recorder while they write letters or read comic books.** In order for lectures to work, you must focus student attention on the material being presented and ensure that they cognitively process the information and integrate it with what they already know.

4. **Students who do not understand the lecture and mechanically write down what the instructor says.** Such students often learn material incorrectly and incompletely because of lack of understanding. In order to make lectures work there has to be some means of checking the accuracy and completeness of students' understanding of the material being presented.

5. **Students who are isolated and alienated and believe that no one cares about them as persons or about their**

academic progress. In order to make lectures work students have to believe that there are other people in the class who will provide help and assistance because they care about them as people and about the quality of their learning.

6. **Entertaining and clear lectures that misrepresent the complexity of the material being presented.** While entertaining and impressing students is nice, it often does not help students understand and think critically about complex material. To make lectures work students must think critically and use higher-level reasoning in cognitively processing course content. One of our colleagues, whom we now team teach with regularly using cooperative learning procedures, is a magnificent lecturer. His explanation of the simplex algorithm for solving linear programming problems is so clear and straightforward that the students go away with the view that it is very simple. Later when they try to solve a problem on their own, they find that they don't have a clue as to how to begin. Our colleague used to blame himself for not explaining well enough. Sometimes he blamed the students. Now he puts small groups of students to work on a simple linear programming problem, circulates and checks the progress of each group and student, provides help where he feels it is appropriate, and only gives his brilliant lectures when the students understand the problem and are ready to hear his proposed solution. Both he and the students are much happier with their increased understanding.

The use of cooperative learning strategies will overcome these enemies by focusing students' attention on academic material, setting a productive learning mood, ensuring that students engage intellectually in the material, keeping students' attention focused on the content, ensuring that misconceptions, incorrect understanding, and gaps in understanding are corrected, providing an opportunity for discussion and elaboration which promote retention and transfer, and by making learning experiences personal and immediate.

Base Groups

Base groups are long term, heterogeneous cooperative learning groups with stable membership whose primary responsibility is to provide support, encouragement, and assistance in making academic progress. The use of base groups tends to improve attendance, personalize the work required and the school experience, and improve the quality and quantity of learning. The base group functions as a support group for the participants that gives support and encouragement for members personally mastering the knowledge, strategies, and skills emphasized in the course and provides feedback on how well they are being learned. They are the source of permanent and caring peer relationships within which students are committed to each other's educational progress. The base group also verifies that each member is completing the assignments and progressing satisfactorily through the academic program. Base groups may also be given the task of letting absent group members know what went on in the class when they miss a session and bring them up to date.

They last for at least a semester, year, or, preferably, for several years. The larger the school and the more complex and difficult the subject matter, the more important it is to have base groups. Learning for your groupmates is a powerful motivator. Receiving social support and being held accountable for appropriate behavior by peers who care about you and have a long-term commitment to your success and well-being is an important aspect of growing up and progressing through school.

At the beginning of each class students meet in their base groups to (1) congratulate each other for living through the day or week (time since the last class) and check to see that none of their group is under undue stress, and (2) review what each member has read since the last class session. Each member should come prepared to give a brief and succinct summary of what he or she has read and thought about. Students often come to class with resources they have found and want to share, or copies of assignments they completed and duplicated for their group members. Occasionally base groups use the beginning time to review for a quiz together to ensure that everyone in the group has read and mastered the assigned material and to assist each other in completing all other course assignments. The major purpose of the base group, however, is to give peer support to students and to increase the probability that students will attend and learn in the class. Base groups may also meet in between class sessions if the teacher wishes and may be given class periods to complete special projects.

It is important that some of the relationships built within cooperative learning groups are permanent. School has to be more than a series of "ship-board romances" that last for only a semester or year. In elementary, junior-high, high-schools, and colleges students should be assigned to permanent base groups. The base groups should then be assigned to most classes so that members spend much of the day together and regularly complete cooperative learning tasks. Doing so will create permanent caring and committed relationships that will provide students with the support, help, encouragement, and assistance they need to make academic progress and develop cognitively and socially in healthy ways.

When used in combination, these formal, informal, and base cooperative learning groups provide an overall structure to classroom life. Of the three, it is the use of formal cooperative learning groups that provides the basis for teachers to gain the expertise in using cooperative learning procedures. Adding the other two enriches the lives of students and their learning and extends the cooperative experience and effects.

At-Risk Students And Permanent Cooperative Relationships

Students who are "at-risk" for dropping out of and/or failing in school are typically in need of caring and committed peer relationships, social support, and positive self-images, as well as higher achievement. These are obtained from cooperative learning experiences. In order to work cooperatively, at-risk students need the social skills required to work effectively with others. Within most classrooms, however, the status quo is either competitive or individualistic instruction within which students are expected to listen to lectures, participate in whole-class discussions, individually complete worksheets without interacting with their classmates, study by themselves, and take the test on Friday.

In this and a number of other ways schools act as if relationships are unimportant. Each semester or year, students get a new set of classmates and a new teacher. The assumption seems to be that classmates and teachers are replaceable parts and any classmate or any teacher will do. The result is that students have a temporary one-semester or one-year relationship with classmates and the teacher.

Relationships do matter. Caring and committed relationships are a major key to school effectiveness, especially for **at-risk** students who often are alienated from their families and society. As early as the 1950's Maccoby found that in low-income neighborhoods where people knew and cooperated with their neighbors, delinquency rates were low, but in similar neighborhoods where people were estranged from one another, delinquency rates were high. She concluded that it was lack of social support and social constraints, not simply poverty, that was the key to delinquency. **Classrooms and schools need to be caring communities in which students care about each other and are committed to each other's well being.**

It is the social support from people who care about you that sparks the commitment to complete assignments, achieve, and advance through school. Dr. David Joyner, for example, when asked the reason the Penn State football teams he played on were so good, stated:

"The reason we were so good, and continued to be so good, was because he (Joe Paterno) forces you to develop an inner

love among the players. It is much harder to give up on your buddy, than it is to give up on your coach. I really believe that over the years the teams I was playing on were almost unbeatable in tight situations. When we needed to get that six inches we got it because of our love for each other. Our camaraderie existed because of the kind of coach and kind of person Joe was."

Through cooperative learning, teachers can create a classroom in which students strive to learn and achieve for their love of each other. Students will care about each other, and become committed to each other's learning and well-being, because of the kind of teacher they have. Camaraderie is created from striving cooperatively to reach mutual goals.

Some of the relationships developed in school need to be permanent. To many "at-risk" students, permanent supportive and caring relationships would increase their achievement and the number of years they spend in school. When groupmates express support and caring, it is more believable and meaningful when the relationships are permanent rather than temporary. When students know that they will spend several years within the same cooperative base group students know that they have to find ways to motivate and encourage their groupmates. Problems in motivating each other to do their schoolwork and achieve cannot be ignored or waited out. In permanent relationships, furthermore, there is increased opportunity to transmit values from achievement-oriented students to "at-risk" peers.

Teacher relationships can also be permanent. If teachers followed students through the grades, continuity in learning and caring could be maintained. Better to be taught 9th-grade English by a 7th-grade English teacher who knows and cares for the students than by an excellent 9th-grade English teacher who does not know and or care about the students.

To build and maintain relationships, individuals must be socially skilled. At-risk students especially need to master the social skills required to work cooperatively with classmates and maintain the relationships formed within cooperative learning groups. These skills often have to be directly taught.

Teaching Students Collaborative Skills

Students who have never been taught how to work effectively with others cannot be expected to do so. Thus, the first experience of many teachers who structure cooperative learning is that their students cannot collaborate with each other. Yet it is within cooperative situations, where there is a task to complete, that social skills become most relevant and should ideally be taught. All students need to become skillful in communicating, building and maintaining trust, providing leadership, and managing conflicts (Johnson, 1986, 1987; Johnson & F. Johnson, 1987). Teaching collaborative skills becomes an important prerequisite for academic learning since achievement will improve as students become more effective in working with each other.

There are two reasons why collaborative skills are directly taught in classrooms where teachers are serious about using cooperative learning. **The first is that interpersonal and small group skills are the engine that powers cooperative learning groups.** For cooperative learning groups to be productive, students must be able to engage in the needed collaborative skills. Without good leadership, effective communication, the building and maintenance of trust, and the constructive resolution of conflicts, cooperative learning groups will not maximize their productivity and effectiveness.

Second, collaborative skills in and of themselves are important instructional outcomes that relate to future career and life success. The importance of cooperative learning procedures goes beyond achievement, positive relationships among diverse students, high self-esteem, and many other important outcomes. The ability of all students to work cooperatively with others is the keystone to building and maintaining stable marriages, families, careers, and friendships. Schooling is future oriented in the sense that the instruction taking place is primarily aimed at preparing students for career and adult responsibilities. The assumption is made that students will be able to apply successfully what they learn in school to career, family, community, and society settings. Being able to perform technical skills such as reading, speaking, listening, writing, computing, and problem solving are valuable but of little use if the person cannot apply technical skills in cooperative interaction with other people in career, family, and community settings. It does no good to train an engineer or secretary, for example, if the person cannot work effectively with other people and contribute what he or she knows to joint efforts and thereby maintain a job as a engineer or secretary after they have finished school. Without some skill in cooperating effectively, it would be difficult (if not impossible) to maintain a marriage, hold a job, or be part of a community, society, and world. Schools have long been places that have promoted unrealistic expectations of what career, family, and community life may be like. Most if not all careers do not expect people to sit in rows and compete with colleagues without interacting with them. The quality of the American work force and the growth of American productivity depends largely on how well citizens can work cooperatively. Teamwork, communication, effective coordination, and divisions of labor characterize most real-life settings. It may be time for schools to more realistically reflect the reality of adult life. Learning how to work cooperatively with others, and knowing how to function as part of a team, may be one of the most important outcomes of schooling.

The interpersonal and small group skills students need to master in order to work cooperatively with peers are detailed elsewhere in **Reaching Out: Interpersonal Effectiveness and Self-Actualization,** (Johnson, 1986), **Human Relations And Your Career,** (Johnson, 1987), and **Joining Together: Group Theory and Group Skills** (Johnson & F. Johnson, 1987). The procedures for teaching students collaborative skills while simultaneously working on academic learning are discussed in **Circles Of Learning** (Johnson, Johnson, and Holubec, 1986).

Summary

Whenever a learning task is assigned, a clear cooperative, competitive, or individualistic goal structure should be given, so that students know how to behave appropriately. While all three goal structures are important and should be used, the dominant goal structure in any class should be cooperative. Any lesson with any age student in any subject area may be taught cooperatively. All it takes is a teacher who is skilled in translating the old competitive and individualistic lessons into cooperative ones. In order to be cooperative, a lesson must include positive interdependence, face-to-face interaction among students, individual accountability, the use of collaborative skills, and the processing of how well the learning groups functioned. These elements must be included in all three types of cooperative learning groups: formal, informal, and base groups. Within formal cooperative learning groups the teacher's role in structuring learning situations cooperatively involves clearly specifying the objectives for the lesson, placing students in learning groups and providing appropriate materials, clearly explaining the cooperative goal structure and the learning task, monitoring students as they work, and evaluating students' performance. Informal cooperative learning groups are used to ensure that students stay intellectually active during lectures. Finally, base groups provide the permanent and long-term relationships that ensure academic progress is made by all students.

When done correctly, cooperative learning tends to promote higher achievement, more positive relationships among students, greater social support, greater self-esteem, as well as many other important instructional outcomes. For cooperative learning groups to be productive, students must be able to engage in the needed leadership, communication, trust-building, and conflict resolution skills. Teaching students the required interpersonal and small group skills can be done simultaneously with teaching academic material. When cooperative groups are functioning at a high level, controversies occur where students disagree as to the answers and conclusions that may be derived from their knowledge and reasoning. Such academic controversies are powerful learning opportunities and the specific procedures are available for structuring cooperative learning groups to ensure that academic conflicts occur and are constructively managed. In order to sustain the long-term implementation and in-classroom help and assistance needed to gain expertise in cooperative learning, teachers need professional support groups made up of colleagues who are also committed to mastering cooperative learning.

Chapter 5

Promoting Teacher's Instructional Expertise

Empowering Teachers Through Cooperative Teams

Human beings regularly accomplish tasks whose complexity exceeds the limitations of individual capacity by cooperating on the different aspects of an otherwise overwhelming task. For an individual, piloting a Boeing 747 is impossible. For a three-person crew, it is straightforward. The crew, furthermore, does not work in isolation. Large numbers of mechanics, service personnel, cabin attendants, air traffic controllers, pilot educators (who keep crew members abreast of the latest developments and sharp in their responses to problem situations), and many others. From the demands of repairing a flat tire on a dark highway ("If you will just hold the flaslight while I...") to the complex requirements of flying a modern passenger jet, teamwork is the most frequent human response to the challenges of coping with otherwise impossible tasks.

Teaching is, in many ways, an impossible job in which to succeed as an individual. The demands are too great, the range of talents required is too varied and broad, the requirements of progressively increasing expertise exceed the capacities of individual staff members. Yet scheduling and incentives are structured to prevent cooperation among staff members. In the "real world" of work cooperation is the norm. Professionals as diverse as nurses, lawyers, newspaper reporters, and football players meet daily in working groups to review their responsibilities, check their progress, solicit ideas for next steps, and design ways to work together on tough problems. Their workplaces are built around recognition of the necessity of team meetings.

Students are not the only people in the school who need to be empowered. Teachers and other staff members can feel just as complacent, helpless and discouraged. Teachers may need to be empowered when they feel:

1. **Complacent and perfectly satistied with the status quo.** "If 70 percent of my students perform above the national norms on standardized tests, why sould I change how I teach?" is an often heard voice of complacency.

2. **Trapped in the status quo.** When teachers believe that they are unable to change from the competitive / individualistic methods of teaching to cooperative learning they need to be reenergized and redirected. Gaining expertise in cooperative learning procedures is hard work and takes some time. Committing the time and effort to increase instructional expertise in using cooperative learning seems impossible to many teachers who have families of their own and family and community responsibilities beyond their teaching.

3. **Overstressed.** Teachers often feel stress in dealing with large classes, undisciplined and unruly students, and difficult teaching conditions.

4. **Lonely, isolated, and alienated.** Many teachers feel rejected and disliked by their colleagues.

5. **Overloaded and overextended.** When teachers are given responsibility for teaching a wide variety of students more complex material at a more rapid rate, managing mainstreaming and desegregation, and preventing delinquency, drug abuse, and sucicide, many feel overloaded and overextended.

6. **Unable to influence the important decisions made in the school.**

The way in which the complacency, helplessness, and discouragement may be reduced is by providing increased social support through cooperative teams. It is a person's colleagues who will be able to show that the status quo is not good enough. It is a person's colleagues who will be able to problem solve the barriers to using cooperative learning. Staff members are empowered through teamwork. Cooperative teams empower their members by making them feel strong, capable, and committed. It is social support from and accountability to peers that motivates committed efforts to implement cooperative learning. If schools are to be places where staff members care about each other and are committed to each other's success, a cooperative structure must exist. To understand how to empower staff members through cooperative teams you must understand the process of gaining expertise in using cooperative learning.

Promoting The Development And Maintenance Of Expertise

Many schools are scarred by competition among teachers. The competition typically makes teachers feel insecure, isolated, cold, reserved, defensive, and competitive in their relationships with fellow teachers and administrators. Feelings of hostility, guardedness, and alienation toward the rest of the school staff create anxiety in teachers, which in turn decreases their effectiveness in the classroom. The teachers act as though they never need help from their colleagues. A fiction is maintained that a "professional and highly trained teacher" has already achieved sufficient competence and skill to handle all classroom situations alone. **The actual result, however, is that innovative and creative teaching is stifled by insecurity, anxiety, and competitiveness.** And the school environment is depressing and discouraging.

All that is changed by having teachers work together cooperatively to get the job done. One of the most constructive contributions you can make to your school is to encourage cooperation among teachers and the use of cooperative learning in the classroom. **In order to maximize the productivity of the school, you want almost every teacher in the school to:**

1. Be able to take any lesson in any subject area and structure it cooperatively.

2. Use cooperative learning at the routine-use level where it is implemented automatically without a great deal of conscious thought or planning. Cooperative learning is a central part of teachers' professional identity and there is a willingness to share their expertise with interested colleagues.

3. Use cooperative learning at least 60 percent of the time. A cooperative context needs to dominate the classroom and school. At least 60 percent of a student's day should be spent in cooperative learning activities. Up to 40 percent of instruction may be individualistic and competitive learning activities.

In order to commit the effort required to gain such expertise in the use of cooperative learning (which usually takes from one to two years of hard work) teachers need considerable support and help from colleagues. Gaining expertise is not a solitary activity. It is a social process requiring a collegial support group. There must be as much cooperation among teachers as there is in the class-room. **How do you structure cooperation among teachers?** The process is the same as for implementing cooperation among students. Having teachers work together to get the job done is structured by:

1. Organizing teachers into colleagial support groups, task for-ces, and ad hoc decision-making groups and, for each group, you establish cooperative goals that all involved teachers wish to accomplish and that require interdependence and interaction among the teachers.

2. Scheduling time for the groups to meet and discuss their work face-to-face. Help and assistance needs to be given and received.

3. Ensuring each group member's contributions are visible enough for a sense of personal responsibility and account-ability to be experienced.

4. Ensuring teachers have the basic communication, trust building, decision-making, and controversy skills to func-tion effectively as a team member.

5. Having the teams periodically discuss how effectively they are functioning and how they can be even better in the fu-ture.

These basic elements of a good cooperative team (i.e., positive interdependence, face-to-face promotive interaction, individual ac-countability, social skills, and group processing) are discussed in detail in Chapter 4.

The major purpose of challenging, inspiring, organizing, model-ing, and encouraging is to ensure that staff members become in-volved in a continual process of increasing their professional expertise. **The most important responsibility of leaders is to promote the development and maintenance of instructional ex-pertise by teachers.** This is accomplished through structuring colleagial support groups whose primary mission is to improve members' competence in implementing cooperative learning within their classrooms. Cooperative learning is the most important instructional strategy from an administrator point of view because of its impact on discipline, school management, and teachers' ability to work effectively with each other. In this chapter the nature of expertise, how it is gained and maintained, and the process of professional growth are discussed. The leader's role in structuring colleagial support groups is then delineated in the next chapter.

Procedural Learning

Knowing is not enough; we must apply. Willing is not enough; we must do.

Goethe

One learns by doing the thing; for though you think you know it, you have no certainty until you try.

Sophocles

"The hand is the cutting edge of the mind."

Jacob Bronowski, **Ascent Of Man**

Increasing instructional (and administrative) expertise requires procedural learning. Learning how to implement cooperative learning is very similar to learning how to play tennis or golf, how to perform brain surgery, or how to fly an airplane. It involves more than simply reading material for a recognition-level or even a total-recall-level of mastery. **Procedural learning** exists when teachers study cooperative learning to:

1. Learn conceptually what cooperative learning is and how it may be appropriately structured and used.

2. Translate their conceptual understanding into a set of operational procedures appropriate for their students and subject areas.

3. Actually use cooperative learning.

4. Eliminate errors in using cooperative learning to move through the initial awkward and mechanical stages of mastery to attain a routine-use, automated level of mastery.

In other words, the teachers being trained must develop a conceptualization of the process of implementing cooperative learning, engage in guided practice to enact the process and eliminate implementation errors, and persevere in using cooperative learning so that they can appropriately use it in a more and more automated fashion.

Procedural learning differs from simply learning facts and acquiring knowledge due to a heavier reliance on feedback about performance and the modification of implementation efforts until the errors of performance are eliminated. Procedural learning involves a progressive refinement of knowledge and skill as the procedures and practiced, practiced, and practiced.

It is the procedural nature of mastering how to implement cooperative learning that makes training teachers different from teaching in the classroom. This may seem strange at first. Traditionally, in the United States, we have made a separation between "head" learning and "hand" learning. "Real" classes are supposed to be head learning while "vocational" classes are supposed to be hand learning. Thus, there is a focus on the head and a denial that the hand is present and important. In training teachers to implement cooperative learning, however, you should remember Jacob Bronowski's (**Ascent of Man**) observation that it is the "hand" that drives the subsequent evolution of conceptual understanding. The "hand" becomes an instrument of vision, revealing the conceptual nature of the procedure being used. To "understand" you have to "do." True understanding only results from doing. **It is from teaching lessons structured cooperatively that teachers will gain an understanding of what cooperative learning is and how powerful it can be.**

In order for teachers to implement cooperative learning procedures to a routine-use level (where they can automatically structure a lesson cooperatively without a great deal of preplanning) they need time to gain experience in an incremental step-by-step manner. Adoption of a new teaching practice requires substantial shifts in habits and routines. These shifts take time. Teachers should not be expected to be immediate experts on cooperative learning or else they will feel overwhelmed and unable to cope. When teachers are expected to gain expertise in too short a period of time "role overload" and feelings of helplessness may result. When given enough time, teachers will experience increased confidence in their professional competence. One to two years may be the average amount of time required to become a skilled user of cooperative learning procedures.

Gaining and maintaining expertise depends on adopting an attitude of experimentation, the fine-tuning of instructional strategies and procedures to integrate them into the teacher's style and situation, and the overcoming of roadblocks to implementation. Without experimentation, fine-tuning, and overcoming roadblocks, no new teaching practice can be implemented.

An Attitude Of Experimentation

Fred and Ralph are both junior high school English teachers. They recently attended a workshop on cooperative learning and became excited about trying it. On the same day, they both taught a grammar lesson structured so that students would work together in cooperative learning groups. Although the lesson went fairly well, it became apparent that many of their students lacked the necessary social skills to work effectively with classmates. Both teachers were disappointed and somewhat taken-aback about the amount of work required to use cooperative learning with their students. Fred thought to himself, "That did not go so well--cooperative learning does not work too well and it will be some time before I try it again." Ralph thought to himself, "That did not work so well--what can I change to improve my implementation of cooperative learning and how soon can I try it again?" Ralph has an attitude of experimentation, Fred does not.

To develop expertise teachers must be seeking it. If teachers are not seeking enhanced expertise, then their expertise is declining. Seeking expertise requires an attitude of experimentation. An **attitude of experimentation** is an orientation toward continually varying one's behavior in order to (1) fine-tune and refine present competencies and (2) try out new strategies that hold some promise of being more effective than current ones. Effective school staffs will be dominated by the attitude of experimentation. Much of what the principal does is aimed at promoting the attitude of experimentation within the school. An attitude of experimentation means that teachers will:

1. **Believe that teaching is a continuous process of developing more effective procedures through modifying old procedures and integrating new ones into one's standard practices.** The continuous improvement of teaching expertise becomes both a personal and professional commitment.

2. **Accept barriers and problems as a natural aspect of modifying teaching procedures** (as opposed to believing they are proof that the new procedures will not work). Innovating always carries the risk of failure and of meeting problems and roadblocks. In highly innovative organizations there is a very high failure rate because new things are constantly being tried out.

3. **View problems and roadblocks as signs that adjustments are needed in the implementation** (as opposed to defeat or failure). Problems and roadblocks need to be viewed as temporary barriers rather than as permanent obstacles. Learning from one's mistakes is a talent found in teachers who continuously improve their teaching competence.

Teachers must choose between risking short-term failure to improve their expertise in using cooperative learning procedures or guaranteeing long-term failure by continuing the status quo within their classrooms. The key to trying cooperative learning out is the willingness to take short-term risks to improve one's professional expertise. **Without risk there is no gain.** If teachers challenge their competence in implementing cooperative learning, they will fail about 50 percent of the time in making the lesson everything they wanted it to be. Teachers who are afraid to risk failure by definition become long-term failures as their strategies and procedures become outdated, inappropriate, and obsolete.

In order to gain expertise in cooperative learning, the teacher must first try it out. Such experimentation involves the risk of short-term failure, for the first few times cooperative learning is used the results may be less than ideal. Even if the first attempts at implementing cooperative learning are very successful, sooner or later teachers will run into roadblocks and barriers and will be tempted to go back to their previous lecture/worksheet approach to teaching. You, the leader, will wish to keep teachers focused on the long-term journey toward increased expertise rather than on the short-term avoidance of failure. Whenever a teacher becomes discouraged or disappointed with a lesson, the question you should ask the teacher is, "What can be learned from the experience?" You may want to remind them that the best teachers of teaching are **trial** and **error**.

Teachers need to be innovative, creative, and persistent in their efforts to increase their expertise. That involves risk. Risk makes people feel uncomfortable. You, the leader, will have to encourage teachers to challenge their competencies, take risks in experiment-ing with new instructional strategies, and move to the edge of their comfort zone. Being in the middle of their "comfort zone" is an un-fortunate place to be. The teachers who are at the edge of their comfort zone will feel the most alive and energized. They are the innovators who are taking risks in increasing their teaching com-petence. Ideally, teachers will be deliberate, systematic, reflective, and thoughtful in taking risks to increase their competence and ex-pertise. One way to ensure that appropriate risk-taking takes place is to organize teachers into colleagial groups.

Teachers committed to increasing their instructional expertise will view failure as an essential ingredient of growth and improve-ment rather than as something shameful that should be hidden. This is a critical aspect of having a willingness to experiment to develop further expertise. There is a myth in our society that teachers must succeed the first time they try something or else they are no good at it and no good as a person. Teachers learn anything (tennis or teaching) by making an effort and recording the success or failure of that effort, and changing the effort accordingly. Failure indicates a need for "fine-tuning" and "tinkering." It does not reflect a lack of ability or effort. **Remember**: "You gotta make the deposits before you can collect the interest, you gotta study the lessons before you can ace the test, you gotta make the call before you make the sale!"

Overcoming Roadblocks And Barriers To Implementation

A **roadblock** is a hurdle that causes temporary difficulties in reaching a goal. A roadblock can be external (such as a student being unwilling to share knowledge with classmates), or internal (such as teachers being uncomfortable if they do not implement cooperative learning perfectly the first time they try it).

One of the most common roadblocks is a natural resistance to change on the part of oneself and one's colleagues, students, and parents. Change almost always creates anxiety. The status quo, even with all its problems, often seems safer and preferable to the unknown consequences of changing current procedures and practices. Other roadblocks to implementing cooperative learning successfully are the teacher not implementing positive interdependence clearly and specifically enough, the students not having the collaborative skills needed, and colleagues, administrators, parents, and students not understanding the power and importance of cooperative learning.

Another barrier to implementation is that teachers are expected never to fail and, if they do, they are expected to deny and hide it because it is viewed competitively as something shameful and as proof that they are incompetent (or less competent than other teachers). Teachers, in other words, are placed in a "bind" where they are supposed to be innovative but also supposed to master magically all new instructional strategies and implement them perfectly the first time they try. The results of this professional bind is a **"binge or starve" approach to teaching**. Either everything is new (binge on innovating) or nothing is new (starve innovation to death). What is needed instead is the controlled, systematic integration of new instructional strategies into current practice.

Gaining Expertise In Using Cooperative Procedures

Expertise is not a substance that can be transmitted or poured by one person into another person. Expertise is gained through appreticeship. Appretices learn how to conduct cooperative lessons in a busy school surrounded by masters and other aprrentices, all engaged in using cooperative learning at varying levels of expertise. From the beginning, teachers/apprentices are expected to use cooperative learning to increase their students' achievement. In understanding how apprenticeship learning operates, it may be helpful to review the apprenticeship systems of the crafts. There is never one master and one apprentice. There is always a group of apprentices who are at varying levels of expertise. Some may be skilled apprentices about to become masters in their own right. Some may be just beginning. Many others are in between. The more experienced apprentices teach the less experienced. They all work together, sharing knowledge, procedures, insights, and solutions to common problems. Thus, cooperative learning is best mastered in a colleagial support group consisting of several teachers who are at different levels in gaining expertise in implementing cooperative learning in their classrooms.

For the most part, teachers teach each other how to use cooperative learning procedures and sustain each other's interest in doing so. When teachers are asked to identify their primary source of innovative ideas about teaching and their primary source of support and assistance, their response is usually, "Other teachers." Learning from colleagues usually takes place both informally through chance meetings in the hallway or teachers' lounge and formally through colleagial support groups.

Procedural learning assumes that a "progressive refinement" of conceptually understanding cooperative learning and the procedures required to use it in the classroom will take place. Teachers progressively refine their competence in using cooperative learning by:

1. **Understanding conceptually what cooperative learning is and how it may be implemented in their classrooms.**

2. **Trying cooperative learning out in their classrooms with their students.** Teachers must be willing to take risks by experimenting with new instructional and managing strategies and procedures. Teachers risk short-term failure to gain long-term success in increasing their expertise by experimenting with new strategies and procedures. It is as-

sumed that one's efforts will fail to match an ideal of what one wishes to accomplish for a considerable length of time until the new strategy is overlearned to a routine-use, automated level.

3. **Assessing how well cooperative learning lessons went and obtaining feedback on one's teaching from others.** Although the lesson may have not gone well, from the progressive refinement point of view failure never occurs. There are simply approximations of what one wants and with refining and fine-tuning of procedures and more practice the approximations get successively closer and closer to the ideal.

4. **Reflecting on what one did and how it may be improved.** The discrepancy between the real and the ideal is considered and plans are made about altering one's behavior in order to get a better match in the future.

5. **Trying cooperative learning out again in a modified and improved way.** Perseverence in using cooperative learning again and again and again is required until the teacher can teach a cooperative lesson routinely and without conscious planning or thought. Even at this point feedback should be attained, reflection on how to improve the implementation of cooperation, and refining and fine-tuning should take place until the teacher retires (or beyond).

As part of gaining expertise in using cooperative learning, teachers must:

1. **Take ownership of cooperative learning** and incorporate it into their professional identity. The more teachers use cooperative learning, and the more effort they expend implementing cooperative learning, the greater their feelings of success and the greater their ownership of cooperative learning.

2. **Train a colleague.** Expertise is never fully attained until one teaches what one knows to someone else.

Teachers do not become proficient in using cooperative learning procedures from attending a workshop or from reading this book. **Teachers become proficient and competent from doing.** For teachers to develop the expertise in cooperative learning procedures they need to structure a cooperative lesson routinely without conscious planning or thought, they have to use cooperative learning procedures frequently and regularly for several years. **Progressive refinement is not something you do once, it is a way of life!**

Gaining An Initial Conceptual Understanding

Two requirements for implementing cooperative learning are that teachers clearly understand what cooperative learning is and have concrete strategies and specific skills to implement cooperative learning in their classrooms.

Teachers gain a conceptual understanding of what cooperative learning is by experiencing/participating in a cooperative lesson, listening to an explanation of how to conduct a cooperative lesson, and watching others demonstrate/model how to conduct a cooperative lesson. Reading about cooperative learning and listening to a lecture about cooperative learning provide some understanding of it. But such a "knowledge-telling" program renders key aspects of expertise invisible to teachers. **A clearer conceptualization of cooperative learning is provided by participating in a cooperative lesson and then watching experts conduct cooperative lessons while explaining the component elements and skills.** Such a conceptual understanding has a number of important functions:

1. It provides teachers with an **advance organizer** for their initial attempts to structure a lesson cooperatively.

2. It provides an internalized guide for the period of relatively independent practice by successive approximations.

3. It provides an interpretative structure for making sense of the feedback, hints, and corrections given during interactive work sessions.

4. It encourages autonomy in reflecting on how their use of cooperative learning compares with the experts' use.

5. It serves as an internal model of expert performance and thus is the basis for development of self-monitoring and self-correcting skills.

Teachers need to build a conceptual understanding of cooperative learning before they try executing a cooperative lesson. To give teachers such a conceptual understanding, the leader:

1. Conducts a lesson structured cooperatively so that teachers can **experience** firsthand what it is like to participate in a cooperative learning session.

2. Explains the components of a cooperative lesson while **modeling / demonstrating** how a lesson is conducted.

A key component for building a conceptual model is observing a demonstration of how to conduct cooperative learning lessons (**Watch me try it**). Such demonstration lessons may first take place in the experienced teacher's classroom and then take place in the novice teacher's classroom. Generally, each demonstration will involve a preconference to discuss the lesson, teaching the lesson while the teacher(s) observes, a postconference in which the lesson is analyzed, and a discussion of how the lesson could be improved next time it is taught. During the preconference the experienced teacher will need to be clear about the **objectives** for the demonstration, a one page **orientation sheet** to precue the observers as to what to expect and look for, agreement on the **observing teacher's role** during the lesson, and a time and place set for

debriefing, that is, discussing the lesson afterwards. During the demonstrations the basic elements of a good cooperative lesson should be emphasized: positive interdependence, promotive (face-to-face) interaction, individual accountability, collaborative skills, and group processing.

Teachers being trained need to observe a number of different people conducting cooperative lessons. Observing a number of colleagues at various stages of mastering the effective use of cooperative learning strategies helps the teachers being trained to develop a conceptual model of what "good" cooperative learning is.

Observing others conduct cooperative lessons is not a stage. It should be a continuous activity for a number of years. The conceptual model is continually updated through further observation. Teachers need continual access to models of expertise-in-use against which to refine their understanding of how to implement cooperative learning. **Having access to several experts and thus to a variety of models of cooperative learning helps teachers understand that there are multiple ways of implementing cooperative learning and that no one individual embodies all knowledge or expertise.** Finally, having opportunities to observe other teachers at varying degrees of skill in using cooperative learning encourages teachers to view learning as an incrementally staged process, while providing them with concrete benchmarks for their own progress.

Trying It Out: Conducting Cooperative Lessons

To understand you have to do. Effective training needs to allow teachers to adapt cooperative learning to their own subject areas, curriculum materials, circumstances, and students. Teachers translate their initial conceptual understanding of cooperative learning into lessons they structured cooperatively. This is done in a series of steps:

1. Engaging in guided practice with coaching and scaffolding that is gradually reduced as they become more and more proficient in planning and conducting lessons structured cooperatively.

2. Engaging in guided practice while explaining out loud how to plan and conduct cooperative learning lessons.

3. Engaging in independent practice while monitoring and correcting their own implementation efforts.

4. Engaging in independent practice in implementing cooperative learning in new subject areas and with new classes.

Teachers have to engage in **guided practice** in using cooperative learning in order to confront and eliminate the obstacles to their initial use. To learn any new instructional procedure and/or skill, teachers have to engage in considerable practice during and immediately following training. It takes about 30 practice sessions before teachers may be fully comfortable in teaching a cooperative lesson. Many of these practice sessions should occur in the presence of members of their colleagial support group.

Helping colleagues to gain expertise in the use of cooperative learning requires ensuring that they engage in successive approximations of expert use with guidance and assistance. While working with colleagues with various levels of expertise in using cooperative learning, teachers engage in a **progressive refinement** process that involves conducting a cooperative lesson, assessing how well it went, reflecting on how to do it better, and conducting a second cooperative lesson, assessing how well it went, and so forth. Through this process of engaging in successive approximations of cooperative learning they gain increasing skill in using cooperative learning and conceptual understanding of what it is and how it works. Mistakes and imperfections in implementation are to be expected and are utilized for increased understanding and a source of insight into how to refine cooperative learning procedures for the specific situation of the teacher.

There are four levels of practice. The **first** level of guided practice consists of the teachers practicing successive approximations of conducting cooperative lessons while colleagues provide prompts, hints, and guidance (i.e., **scaffolding**) on how to do so. When teachers begin the procedure of learning how to structure learning situations cooperatively through successive approximations, cognitive scaffolding is provided to move teachers closer and closer to expert use of cooperative learning. **Scaffolding** is support, in the form of reminders, prompts, and help, that the teachers require to approximate the expert use of cooperative learning. Teachers should receive as much support as they need to structure the lesson cooperatively and no more. This support consists of giving **prompts** that help the teachers structure the situation cognitively, and thus be able to take the next step in performing the procedures of using cooperatively learning. Prompts serve to simplify the complex process of elaborating and reconsidering the teachers' plans by suggesting specific lines of thinking for the teachers to follow. **Typical prompts are suggestions that include limited options:**

1. For this lesson you need both an academic objective and a social skills objective. How would you like to state each?

2. In terms of group size, it is better to start small. Would you prefer groups of two, three, or four?

3. You may decide who is in each group or you may assign students to groups randomly. Which would you prefer to do?

4. Cooperative learning begins with positive goal interdependence. How do you want to state the cooperative goal?

5. In addition to positive goal interdependence there are other ways of saying "sink or swim together." Would you like to assign roles or arrange materials in a jigsaw?

6. A good cooperative lesson includes individual accountability. This may be structured either by having each stu-

dent take an individual test or randomly pick students to answer for their groups. Which would you prefer to do in this lesson?

7. There are a number of social skills that would be helpful in achieving your academic objectives. Which ones would you like to emphasize and observe for in this lesson?

8. Groups improve when they process how well members are working together. How would you like to manage group processing in this lesson?

As the teachers continue to conduct cooperative lessons, the help, guidance, prompts, and hints are **faded** as they are no longer needed. Once the teachers have a grasp of how to structure a lesson cooperatively, colleagues reduce their participation (**fade**), providing only limited hints, refinements, and feedback to the teachers, who practice by successively approximating smooth execution of the whole process of structuring lessons cooperatively. Teachers plan and present cooperative lessons using the prompts by themselves, a process called **soloing**. This enables teachers to assume both the producer and the prompter roles, that is, to monitor and correct themselves as they become more skillful in using cooperative learning.

The **second** level of guided practice consists of teachers practicing cooperative lessons while **articulating and explaining** out loud how to do so to their colleagues. This ensures that the scaffolding is internalized and **self-monitoring** and **self-correcting** of how to structure cooperative lessons takes place.

The **third** level is independent practice. Teachers conduct cooperative lessons while **self-monitoring** and **self-correcting** their efforts. In effect, instead of receiving feedback from others as to how well a cooperative lesson has been implemented, teachers give themselves feedback. This solidifies their sense of **self-efficacy** and **commitment** to implement cooperative learning in their classrooms. The teachers you work with must **persevere** in doing so.

Finally, teachers must expand and extend their use of cooperative learning. Teachers typically pick one subject area, class, or unit to implement cooperative learning. They concentrate on using cooperative learning within that context. Over time teachers need to be encouraged to use cooperative learning in more and more complex ways and in more diverse and different subject areas and situations (i.e., the use of cooperative learning needs to be **decontextualized**).

The interplay between observation, guided practice with scaffolding, increasing independent practice, and extending one's use of cooperative learning aids teachers both in developing self-monitoring and self-correcting skills, and in integrating the skills and conceptual knowledge needed to advance toward expertise in the use of cooperative learning procedures.

A colleagial support group is essential for trying cooperative learning out. **To gain expertise in using cooperative learning teachers must engage in "hands on" and "job embedded" efforts with "on call" help and support when they need it.** Colleagues who can provide support and assistance should be on call to demonstrate, co-teach, give feedback, problem solve, and provide help when it is needed and wanted.

Assessing How Well Cooperative Learning Was Implemented

The key to assessing the consequences of one's experimentation with cooperative learning is the realization that one can never fail. Rather, one's behavior approximates what one ideally wishes, and through practice and the process of progressive refinement the approximation gets successively closer and closer to the ideal. **You have to sweat in practice before you can perform in concert!**

Short-term failure is part of the process of gaining expertise and long-term success is inevitable when short-term failure is followed by persistent practice, obtaining feedback, and reflecting on how to implement cooperative learning more competently. Failure needs to be accepted as an inevitable result of experimentation and a source of learning about improving teaching practices. This is easier to do when you are part of a colleagial support group. Feedback is best obtained from others. Gaining expertise takes "learning partners" who are willing to trust each other, talk frankly about their teaching, and observe each other's performance over a prolonged period of time and help each other identify the errors being made in implementing cooperative learning. Unless one is willing to reveal lack of expertise to obtain accurate feedback, expertise cannot be gained. In other words, **the progressive refinement inherent in procedural learning requires a cooperative relationship among colleagues.**

Reflecting On How Implementation Of Cooperation May Be Improved

The key to reflection is having colleagues to help you do it. Teachers need to reflect jointly with supportive colleagues about implementation efforts. Insights are most frequently obtained in response to questions (remember Socrates) and in explaining why you did what you did to nonevaluative and supportive peers. Jointly reflecting on the implementation of cooperative learning with supportive and interested colleagues provides continuous and immediate feedback on quality of implementation, assistance in developing lessons and materials,

and help in solving problems and overcoming barriers. **You have to explain to understand.**

In order to perfect and expand the use of cooperative learning strategies teachers need a colleagial support group whose goal is to promote the continuous growth in competence in using cooperative learning. The procedures for structuring teacher colleagial support groups will be covered in the next chapter.

Fine-Tuning Instructional Practices

One of the most important findings of the research on innovation in schools from the 1950's, 1960's, and 1970's is that curriculum packages are quickly adopted in schools and then quickly discontinued. **Lasting implementation seems to require that teachers "reinvent" the teaching practice for themselves.** Teachers may reinvent cooperative learning by adopting it to their style, personality, students, and school, and by "fine-tuning" the procedures for using cooperative learning until there is a good fit between them and the other teaching strategies the teachers use. Although a lesson may have gone well, it is never a failure as it is simply an approximation of what the teacher wanted. With refining and fine-tuning the approximations get successively closer and closer to the ideal. How cooperative learning is implemented, furthermore, must match the teacher's situation. Different teachers, for example, structure positive interdependence differently (some through bonus points, some through divisions of labor, some through jigsawing materials, and some through group grades). The procedures selected for creating positive interdependence have to be compatible with a teacher's teaching philosophy and methods. The teachers who are most likely to make cooperative learning a part of their daily teaching are those who make it their own.

As the teachers being trained persevere and gain more and more expertise in planning and conducting cooperatively structured lessons, the ownership of cooperative learning must switch from the instructional leader to them. They must begin to believe and feel that it is **their cooperative learning** they are doing, not someone else's. Successes must be theirs, not yours. As you work with them, be sure to attribute the cause of successes to their efforts and understanding, not to your help and assistance. Give them the credit, take any blame. Promote their belief that they are competent and knowledgeable in implementing cooperative learning (i.e., self-efficacy) when it is appropriate to do so.

Teaching What One Learns To Colleagues

It is only when we develop others that we permanently succeed.

Harvey S. Firestone

Nothing is completely learned until it is taught to someone else. The process of thinking how to communicate what one is learning to another person results in greater higher-level reasoning than does learning something strictly for one's own use. The actual teaching of someone else of what one knows results in more deeper-level understanding and greater insight into cooperative learning than does using cooperative learning in isolation from others. A major function of colleagial support groups is to provide a forum within which teachers may explain to colleagues how they are implementing cooperative learning and teach their colleagues how to do likewise.

Summary

The most important responsibility leaders have is to promote professional expertise within the school staff. To do so requires an understanding of the process by which expertise is attained and maintained. Increasing professional expertise begins with an understanding of (1) procedural learning, (2) the attitude of experimentation, and (3) the process and gaining and maintaining expertise.

Procedural learning exists when teachers learn conceptually what cooperative learning is and translate their conceptual understanding into a set of operational procedures appropriate for their students and subject areas. The operational procedures then need to be used and the errors of initial use need to be eliminated until the teacher has attained a routine-use, automated level of mastery.

Procedural learning requires teachers to **progressively refine** their conceptual understanding of cooperation and ability to conduct cooperatively structured lessons. Teachers have to conduct a cooperative lesson, assess how well it went, reflect on how to do it better, and then conduct a second cooperative lesson, repeating this process over and over again with both persistence and creativity. Doing so begins with teachers having an **attitude of experimentation**, trying out variations of cooperative learning, believing that teaching is a continuous process of developing more effective procedures through modifying old procedures and integrating new ones into one's standard practices. As teachers use cooperative learning they **fine-tune** their skills in doing so and face and overcome the roadblocks and barriers that arise any time new teaching practices are implemented.

There are four steps in gaining expertise in the use of cooperative learning (as well as in any other competency). The **first** is attaining an initial conceptual understanding of cooperative learning by participating in a cooperative lesson, listening to an explanation of how to conduct cooperative lessons, and watching others demonstrate and model how to conduct a cooperative lesson. The **second** step is trying it out by translating initial conceptual understanding into a set of operational procedures by engaging in guided practice followed by independent practice and increasing the use of cooperative learning until it is used most of the school day. The **third** step is when teachers take ownership of cooperative learning and incorporate it into their professional identity. The **fourth** step is finding a colleague to train. Expertise is never fully attained until one teaches what one knows to someone else.

Expertise is not gained in isolation from colleagues. Gaining and maintaining expertise is an interpersonal process that requires supportive and encouraging colleagues who help one assess the consequences of cooperative lessons, model and explain how to conduct cooperative lessons, provide prompts and hints on how to do so effectively, analyze how specific lessons may be improved, and celebrate one's successes in increasing one's professional competence. The nature of colleagial support groups is discussed in the next chapter.

Chapter 6

Structuring Colleagial Support Groups

Effective Colleagial Learning

For things we have to learn before we can do them, we learn by doing them.

Aristotle

To lead your school you need to challenge the status quo of competitive-individualistic learning and staff relations, inspire a new vision of cooperative learning and cooperation among staff members, empower staff members by organizing them into cooperative teams, lead by example by using cooperative strategies and procedures, and encourage staff members to persevere until they have gained considerable expertise in using cooperative learning. **The most important aspect of leadership is empowering your staff by organizing them into cooperative teams.** And of the three types of teams, the most important are colleagial support groups in which teachers help and assist each other to improve their teaching competence. All staff efforts within schools should be aimed directly or indirectly at educating students. There is no doubt that teachers teach better when they experience support from their peers.

It is time that the school became a modern organization. In the real world, most of the important work is done by cooperative teams rather than by individuals. For example, the development of most computer systems requires highly interactive groups of knowledgeable workers. Similarly, the number of people coauthoring scientific papers has increased dramatically in recent years. In 1986, 75 people co-authored a paper with evidence related to the location of the gene for Duchenne muscular dystrophy. Instead of requiring teachers to engage in quiet and solitary performance in individual classrooms, teachers should be organized into cooperative teams with an emphasis on seeking and accepting help and assistance from peers, soliciting constructive criticism, and negotiating by articulating their needs, discerning what others need, and discovering mutually beneficial outcomes. Modernizing the school requires that teachers work in cooperative teams as most other adults in our society do.

When teachers are isolated and alienated from their peers, they will also tend to be alienated from their work and, therefore, not likely to commit a great deal of psychological energy to their jobs or commit themselves to grow professionally by attaining increased expertise.

Colleagial support groups begin when you, the leader, get two or more teachers to meet together and talk about their efforts to implement cooperative learning. There can be little doubt that teachers' main source of inspiration and creativity is other teachers. When teachers are asked to identify their primary source of innovative ideas about teaching and their primary source of support and assistance, their response is usually "other teachers." In a competitive / individualistic school, learning from colleagues is often informal and takes place through chance meetings in the hallway or teachers' lounge. In a cooperative school, learning from colleagues is formally structured by organizing teachers into colleagial support groups.

Being An Effective Colleague

Traditionally, teachers have not been skilled in working effectively with adult peers. Blake and Mouton (1974) found that teachers and administrators lacked teamwork skills and were too ready to resolve differences by voting or by following the "offical leader." They observed that educators were far less competent in working in small problem-solving groups than were industrial personnel. And they found that educators described themselves as being more oriented toward compromising quality of work for harmonious relationships, exerting minimal effort to get their job done, and being more oriented toward keeping good relationships than toward achieving the school's goals. Blumberg, May, and Perry (1974) found that teachers were ill- equipped behaviorally to function as part of a faculty, as they lacked the skills and attitudes needed for effective group problem-solving.

The lack of competence in being a constructive colleague, however, is not primarily the fault of teachers. The organizational structure of the school traditionally has discouraged colleagiality among teachers and severely limited their opportunities to cooperate with each other. Schools are **loosely coupled** organizations in which teachers and administrators function far more independently than interdependently, with little or no supervision, enagaging in actions that do not determine or affect what others do, and engage in actions that seem isolated from their consequences (Johnson, 1979). Teachers have been systematically isolated from one another during most of the school day. And that isolation has resulted in teachers experiencing an amorphous and diffuse competition with their peers.

Colleagial Support Groups

Willi Unsoeld, a famous mountaineer and philosopher, once said to a group of mountain climbers, *"Pull together...in the mountains you must depend on each other for survival."* Teaching has a lot in common with mountain climbing.

can catch you if you fall. The climber conceptually plans a path up the "first leg" of the cliff, advances along that path, puts in pitons, slips in the rope, and continues to advance until the first leg of the climb is completed. The pitons help the belayer catch the climber if the climber falls and they mark the path up the cliff. The rope, called the "life-line," goes from the belayer through the pitons up to the climber. When the climber has completed the first leg of the climb, the climber becomes the belayer and the belayer becomes the climber. The original belayer advances up the route marked out by the original climber until the first leg is completed, and then leap-frogs by becoming the lead climber for the second leg of the climb. This leap-frog procedure is repeated until the summit is reached.

The similarities of mountain climbing to teaching are:

1. Both are based on a commitment to accomplish something. While a climber may state that it is important to climb a mountain because "it is there," a teacher may state that it is important to teach each student because "he or she is there."

2. Both climbing and teaching involve risking failure. In teaching, failure is risked whenever the teacher tries out and attempts to perfect a new strategy and procedure.

3. It takes two people to make a climb. While it is possible for one person to hike through the mountains, if you want to scale the peaks, you need a partner. The same is true of teaching. To scale the heights, you need a belayer, a supportive colleague, who will catch you if you fall.

4. You climb with your eyes and your brain. Climbing is first and foremost a conceptual activitiy. You pick out your route and then advance. Teaching is also a conceptual activitiy that is thought through in advance and then executed.

5. Reciprocal leadership and followership is needed in climbing. To be a good climber, you must have two sets of competencies. You must be able to **lead** (finding and marking a path up the cliff so that others may easily follow you) and **belay** (providing a secure anchor for those who are climbing). You must mark out a new trail for a period of time and then provide a secure anchor for others to follow, catch up, and mark out a new trail. Then you follow their path until you have caught up to them, leap frog, and mark out a new path for them to follow. There is an ebb and flow of leading and supporting in mountain climbing. The same is true for teaching. Working with colleagues, you develop some expertise in cooperative learning, share it, provide support for their initial use of cooperative learning, and then learn new aspects of using cooperative learning from them in turn.

6. Both climbing and teaching involve trust. You have to be trustworthy in providing support. If your partner falls, you have to be able to catch him. When you are the climber, you have to be trusting of your partner to provide a secure anchor. It is your confidence in your belayer that gives you the courage to risk a difficult climb.

7. Climbers spend a lot of time hanging by their fingers and toes to a cliff, feeling scared, and thinking, "What is the use, I will never make it." Many teachers have similar feelings when facing their classes. When the fear gets too great, a climber becomes "gripped" or "frozen," unable to advance and unable to retreat. A climber in this state has to be rescued by partners.

The success of the school depends on the success teachers have in educating students. The success of teachers in educating students depends on (a) how committed teachers are to continually increasing their instructional expertise and (b) the amount of physical and psychological energy teachers give to their work. The commitment of physical and psychological energy to achieve the goal of improving one's instructional expertise is heavily influenced by the degree to which colleagues are supportive and encouraging. **There is no doubt that teachers teach better when they experience support from their peers.** In most schools, however, such support is hard to achieve. As a result, most teachers feel harried, isolated, and alienated. Yet there is a deep human need to work collaboratively and intimately with supportive people. Colleagial support group meetings provide teachers with the opportunity to share ideas, support each other's efforts to use cooperative learning, and encourage each other.

In the school, the colleagial support group is the climbing team. A **colleagial support group** consists of two to five teachers who have the goal of improving each other's instructional expertise and ensuring each other's professional growth. Colleagial support groups should be small and members should be heterogeneous. **Colleagial support groups are first and foremost safe places where**:

1. Members like to be.

2. There is support, caring, concern, laughter, camaraderie, and celebration.

3. The primary goal of improving each other's competence in using cooperative learning is never obscured.

The purpose of this colleagial support group is to work jointly to improve continuously each other's expertise in using cooperative learning procedures or, in other words, to:

1. Provide the help, assistance, support, and encouragement each member needs to gain as high a level of expertise in using cooperative learning procedures as possible.

2. Serve as an informal support group for sharing, letting off steam, and discussing problems connected with implementing cooperative learning procedures.

3. Serve as a base for teachers experienced in the use of cooperative learning procedures to teach other teachers how to structure and manage lessons cooperatively.

4. Create a setting in which camaraderie and shared success occur and are celebrated.

Colleagial support groups succeed when they are carefully structured to ensure active participation by members and concrete products (such as lesson plans) that members can actually use. The structure must clearly point members toward increasing each other's expertise in implementing cooperative learning to prevent meetings from degenerating into gripe sessions, destructive criticism of each other, amateur therapy, or sensitivity training. Members need to believe they sink or swim together, ensure considerable face-to-face discussion and assistance takes place, hold each other accountable to implement cooperative learning in between meetings, learn and use the interpersonal and small group skills required to make meetings productive, and periodically initiate a discussion of how effective the colleagial support group is in carrying out its mission. Task-oriented discussion, planning, and problem solving, as well as empathy and mutual support, should dominate the meetings.

The three key activities of a colleagial support group are (Little, 1981):

1. Frequent professional discussions of cooperative learning in which information is shared, successes are celebrated, and problems connected with implementation are solved.

2. Coplanning, codesigning, copreparing, and coevaluating curriculum materials relevant to implementing cooperative learning in the classrooms of the members.

3. Coteaching and reciprocal observations of each other teaching lessons structured cooperatively and jointly processing those observations.

Professional Discussions

What teachers need most of all professionally is opportunties to talk to each other about teaching. Within the colleagial support groups there must be frequent, continuous, increasingly concrete and precise talk about the use of cooperative learning procedures. Through such discussion members build a concrete, precise, and coherent shared language that can describe the complexity of using cooperative learning procedures, distinguish one practice and its virtues from another, and integrate cooperative learning procedures into other teaching practices and strategies that they are already using. Through such discussions, teachers will exchange successful procedures and materials. They will focus on solving specific problems members may be having in perfecting their use of cooperative learning strategies. Most of all, teachers' comprehension and deeper-level understanding of the nature of cooperative learning will be enhanced by explaining how they are implementing it to their colleagues.

Joint Planning and Curriculum Design

| *Well begun is half done.*

Aristotle

Members of professional support groups should frequently plan, design, prepare, and evaluate lesson plans together. This results in teachers sharing the burden of developing materials needed to conduct cooperative lessons, generating emerging understanding of cooperative learning strategies, making realistic standards for students and colleagues, and providing the machinery for each other to implement cooperative learning procedures. Teachers should leave each meeting of their colleagial support group with something concrete that helps them implement cooperative learning. The process of planning a lesson together, each conducting it, and then processing it afterwards is often constructive. This cycle of **coplanning, parallel teaching, coprocessing** may be followed by one of **coplanning, coteaching, coprocessing**.

The discussions and coplanning that takes place within colleagial support groups ensures that teachers clarify their understanding of what cooperative learning is and creates a support and accountability system to ensure that they try it out. The next steps in increasing expertise are to assess the consequences of using cooperative learning, reflecting on how well the lesson went, and teaching another cooperative lesson in a modified way. All of these steps benefit from the input and feedback from supportive colleagues. The more colleagues are involved in your teaching, the more valuable the help and assistance they can provide.

Reciprocal Observations

Members of professional support groups should frequently observe each other teaching lessons structured cooperatively and then provide each other with useful feedback. This observation and feedback provide members with shared experiences to discuss and refer to. The observation and feedback, furthermore, have to be reciprocal. **Teachers especially need to treat each other with the deference that shows they recognize that anyone can have good and bad days and that the mistakes they note in a colleague may be the same mistakes that they will make tomorrow.**

We have found a number of important guidelines which we have teachers follow when they are observing the teaching other members of their professional support group. These guidelines include:

1. Realize that you can learn from every other member of the group, regardless of their experience and personal characteristics.

2. Make sure observation and feedback is reciprocal.

3. Ask the person you're observing what he/she would like you to focus your attention on. This may include specific students the teacher may wish observed, specific aspects of structuring interdependence or accountability, or some other aspect of cooperative learning.

4. Focus feedback and comments on what has taken place, not on personal competence.

5. Don't confuse a teacher's personal worth with her/his current level of competence in using cooperative learning procedures.

6. Be concrete and practical in your discussions about how effectively members are using cooperative learning procedures.

7. Above all, communicate respect for each other's overall teaching competence. We all have professional strengths and weaknesses. Recognize and respect those strengths in each other.

There are a number of ways to arrange time and opportunity for observing. The principal can take one teacher's class. If each building administrator taught one period a day, about one-fourth of the teachers would be released for a period each week. Two classes can be combined to view a movie or participate in an instructional activity, freeing one teacher. A class of students can be sent to the computer-lab or library and given research projects to complete. Volunteer aides or student teachers can be recruited to cover classes while teachers work together.

Working collaboratively with others brings with it camaraderie, friendship, warmth, satisfaction, and feelings of success. These are all to be enjoyed.

Helpful Norms

There are a number of helpful norms for professional support groups that will help them function effectively. These norms include:

1. I don't have to be perfect and neither do you!

2. It takes time to master cooperative learning procedures to a routine use level.

3. I'm here to improve my competence in using cooperative learning procedures.

4. You can criticize my implementation of cooperative learning procedures without me taking it personally.

5. I am secure enough to give you feedback about your implementation of cooperative learning procedures.

Structuring Colleagial Support Groups

Take care of each other. Share your energies with the group. No one must feel alone, cut off, for that is when you do not make it."

Willi Unsoeld

Table 6.1

Difference Between PSG's and Traditional Teaming

Professional Support Groups	Traditional Teams
Clear positive goal interdepen- is structured among teachers	Teachers are told to work together
All members share leadership responsibilities	A team leader is assigned
Teachers are trained to function skillfully in collaborative groups	No skill training is provided
High individual accountability	No individual accountability

There are a number of steps that principals need to go through in structuring and managing colleagial support groups aimed at implementing cooperative learning procedures in the classroom. These steps include:

1. Schedule an "awareness" session in which all staff members are informed of the nature and power of cooperative learning.

2. Publicly announce your support for the use of cooperative learning procedures.

3. Specify the "key players" in your school and diagnose their level of commitment to implementing cooperative learning.

4. Recruit and select competent teachers to participate in the colleagial support groups.

5. Study the nature of cooperative learning.

6. Highlight the goal interdependence among members of a colleagial support group.

7. Negotiate a contract among the members of the colleagial support groups and a contract between the groups and you, if appropriate.

8. Convene and structure the first few meetings of the colleagial support group until members are able to structure them by themselves.

9. Provide the resources and incentives needed for the colleagial support groups to function.

10. Observe other members frequently.

11. Celebrate members' successes in implementing cooperative learning.

12. Ensure that the colleagial support groups discuss how well they function and maintain good relationships among members.

13. Build yourself in as a member not out as a consultant.

14. Keep a long-term, developmental perspective and protect the colleagial support groups from other pressures.

15. Be inclusive and include teachers who become interested, not exclusive.

Each of these steps will be discussed in the following sections.

Awareness Session

All members of a school staff need to participate in an awareness session on what cooperative learning is and why it should be implemented. Those teachers who do not use cooperative learning initially will then understand what their colleagues are doing and why. And when cooperative learning comes up in professional conversations and faculty meetings, all staff members will have the same definition and conception of what cooperative learning is.

Announcing Your Support

Forming of teacher colleagial support groups, aimed at improving competencies in using cooperative learning procedures, begins with the "cooperative learning leaders" announcing their support for teachers using cooperative learning strategies. This should take place in staff meetings, PTA meetings, and school newsletters. Such announcements should be frequent and cooperative learning should be described concretely in terms of life in school. The teachers who are using cooperative learning procedures should be visibly and publicly praised. The message that should be given is, "It is proper to structure learning cooperatively and therefore the staff should strive to do so." During the year, give updates on new research or describe new procedures to implement cooperative learning. Describe how cooperative learning agrees with district and school goals. Tolerate and absorb any initial failures of teachers learning how to structure lessons cooperatively. School displays and bulletin boards (as well as banners in the hallways) can be used to promote cooperative learning. An example is an elementary school in which the principal placed a large banner opposite the main door to the school stating, "In this school we help each other learn." It is important that supervisors or principals do not kill cooperative learning by skepticism or neglect.

Specifying "Key Players" and Their Commitment

Consider the members of the school staff and administration. Who are the people whose support is necessary for a long-term, multi-year effort to implement cooperative learning to be launched and maintained in your school? These are the "key players." Identify the key players, rate their level of commitment to implementing cooperative learning, and the level of commitment you need them

to have. Then plan how you will increase their commitment to the level needed.

Recruiting And Selecting Members

In selecting teachers to organize into a colleagial support group, look for teachers who are interested in trying cooperative learning, who will follow through and actually use cooperative learning, and who are your friends or at least teachers you would enjoy working with. Choose staff members who are motivated to use cooperative learning, who are committed enough to persist until the group is successful, and who are supportive, caring, and interpersonally skilled. Individuals who teach next door or across the hall from each other and who are already supporting each other's teaching efforts or are friends are often the best ones to start with.

Teachers can be recruited or selected to participate in colleagial support groups in a number of ways. You will want to look for members who are open, sensitive, supportive, and colleagially competent. Disgruntled, nonconstructive teachers tend to ruin colleagial support groups. Their criticism is rarely productive and they often lack wisdom in choosing battle-grounds. Alienated teachers may also be disruptive and demoralizing. And incompetent teachers who are struggling to survive are unprepared to begin colleagial growth until they gain basic control and self-confidence. In other words, **the members should be hand-picked to make sure the colleagial support groups are successful.** Specific methods of recruiting and selecting members may include:

1. Listening and participating in on teachers' conversations to find out who might be interested in perfecting their skills in using cooperative learning procedures.

2. Bringing teachers who like using cooperative learning procedures together.

3. Recruiting grade level groups that already informally or formally serve as colleagial support groups.

4. Recruiting teachers who are good friends with each other and who will welcome the opportunity to work more close- ly with each other.

5. Recruiting teachers who have the same preparation period.

When recruiting colleagial support group members, approach your staff members very carefully (to establish a collaborative relationship). This is a touchy task as it is easy to drive teachers away. Be sure to present the possibility of working together to im- prove your own use of cooperative procedures as well as theirs. Never say "It is easy" or "Anyone can do it!" Never say, "Have I got a good idea for you! Here is how we are going to change the way you teach!" Instead, ask for help in implementing cooperative learn- ing in the school, use a soft approach of indicating an open door, make the cooperative (not expert-novice) relationship clear, and be clear about the purpose of providing support and assistance in help- ing each other increase expertise in implementing cooperative learning. Be sure to be realistic about the length of time it will take to gain some expertise in using cooperative learning procedures and the amount of work it will take.

Once you have picked two or more teachers and approached them about working together on implementing cooperative learn- ing, they must know how to proceed. In essence, they must know how to help each other develop expertise in implementing coopera- tive learning.

Studying the Nature of Cooperative Learning

When you have established the membership of a colleagial sup- port group, you will find it helpful to review the nature of coopera- tive learning for the members. Methods are:

1. Recommend a training course or workshop they can par- ticipate in.

2. Arrange for them to observe colleagues who are experienced in using cooperative learning procedures.

3. Provide **Circles Of Learning** or **Cooperation in the Classroom** for members to read.

4. Have consultants or experienced teachers present an awareness session for all the staff in the school.

5. Have the group meet with a district specialist in cooperative learning.

The heart of cooperative learning is the five basic elements. Simply placing teachers in small groups does not mean that they will commit themselves to each other's professional growth. Proximity may result in competition to see who is best and in high levels of evaluation apprehension and fear. Cooperative relationships among teachers or administrators have to be structured just as carefully as does cooperative learning in the classroom. This means that the five essential elements of cooperative relationships have to be carefully structured within colleagial support groups (Johnson, Johnson, & Holubec, 1986):

1. **Positive interdependence:** Each member must perceive that it is "sink or swim together."

2. **Face-to-face promotive interaction:** Each member must orally discuss what he or she is learning and promote colleagues' productivity.

3. **Personal responsibility/individual accountability:** Each member must feel personally responsible and accountable for contributing his or her fair share of the work.

4. **Social skills:** Each member must master the basic leadership, communication, decision-making, trust-building, and conflict-management skills necessary for a cooperative group to function effectively.

5. **Group processing:** Each member must periodically reflect on how well the group is functioning and analyze how the interaction among group members can become more productive.

After reviewing the nature of cooperative learning, the level of expertise of each member of the colleagial support group should be assessed. Note the amount of training each member has and discuss the next training course he or she should next attend.

A critical aspect of effective colleagial support groups is how they manage conflict among members. When teachers disagree with each other, a set of specific controversy and conflict-management skills are required to ensure that creative insights and more positive relationships result. These procedures and skills are detailed elsewhere (Johnson, Johnson, & Smith, 1986; Johnson & F. Johnson, 1987).

Highlighting Goal Interdependence

> If a man does not know to which port he is sailing, no wind is favorable.

> Seneca

The goal of a colleagial support group is to work jointly to improve continuously each other's competence in using cooperative learning procedures or, in other words, to teach each other how to better use cooperative learning strategies. Members of a colleagial support group must believe that they need each other and in order to complete the group's task, they "sink or swim together." Ways of creating the perception of positive interdependence are mutual goals, joint rewards, shared materials and information, a division of labor, and a group-space in which to meet and work. Review the chapter on positive interdependence in **Cooperation In The Classroom** and plan how to use at least four of the methods of structuring positive interdependence in planning colleagial support group meetings.

Leaders challenge the status quo of competitive / individualistic teaching and create a mutual vision of cooperative classrooms. By highlighting the mutual goals teachers are striving to achieve and creating a belief that "we sink or swim together," the leader provides meaning, significance, and heroism to teaching. In a General Motors plant a number of years ago the manager put up signs all over the walls saying "Beat Japan" and the like. The manager even enticed some Hell's Angels types into singing "God Bless America" at a plant rally. When there is meaning to what one does, ordinary people exert extraordinary effort. These are methods businesses use to highlight the mutual goals of the employees. Schools need to do likewise. Banners can proclaim that it is a cooperative school in which students help each other learn and teachers help each other provide quality instruction. All individuals need to be working towards meaningful goals. Teachers are willing to commit psychological and physical energy to a cause they perceive to be (in some sense) great. The leader becomes the "keeper of the dream" who inspires staff members to commit effort to quality teaching. It is the cooperative goals that highlight the meaning to what staff members are doing.

Negotiate the Contract

When teachers become part of a colleagial support group they accept certain mutual responsibilities. These include:

1. Attend and actively participate in the meetings of the colleagial support group.

2. Use cooperative learning procedures regularly and frequently in their classes.

3. Help, assist, encourage, and support other members' use of cooperative learning.

These responsibilities need to be made into a contract that is eventually formalized and will serve as a basis for discussing how well the colleagial support group is functioning. The responsibilities of the "cooperative learning leaders" in structuring and managing the colleagial support group need to be clear in order to legitimize their involvement in the group.

Structuring the Initial Meetings

The activities of the colleagial support group are aimed at helping all members master, refine, adapt, and experiment with cooperative learning procedures. Discussing their implementation efforts, jointly planning lessons and jointly designing curriculum materials, and reciprocally observing each other's implementation efforts are the major activities of the group.

The "cooperative learning leader" should schedule and convene the **first meeting of the colleagial support group** and ensure that it covers the following agenda items:

1. Your support of their efforts in implementing cooperative learning procedures.

2. When the regular meeting time will be. The meeting has to last at least 50 to 60 minutes. Breakfast clubs, which meet once a week for breakfast before school begins are popular.

3. The purposes of meetings (discussion of implementation efforts, joint planning of lessons and materials, and reciprocal observation).

4. An assessment of the resources they need in order to meet regularly and engage in these activities. Potential resources are discussed in the next section.

5. Plans to make each meeting both productive and fun. With that in mind you might ask who is going to be in charge of

the refreshments for the next meeting (a cooperative effort is recommended).

6. Specific plans for:

   a. When the next meeting will be.

   b. What cooperatively structured lessons they will teach before the next meeting.

   c. What the agenda for the next meeting will be (one item will be to discuss how well their cooperatively structured lessons went).

7. Agree on a tentative contract among members and between the group and yourself.

A sample agenda for the second meeting is:

1. Welcome everyone and have a "warm-up," such as a hand-out on the types of positive interdependence that may be used in cooperatively structured lessons.

2. Discuss their use of cooperative learning procedures:

   a. Lessons taught during the past week.

   b. Their successes--what were the things they liked best.

   c. Any problems that surfaced during the lessons.

3. Discuss the problems at some length and generate a number of alternative strategies for solving each, so that each member may select from a menu of alternative solutions rather than having to implement any one solution.

4. Jointly plan a lesson that they will all teach during the following week.

5. Plan the agenda and menu for the next meeting.

A sample agenda for the third meeting may be:

1. Warm up by handing out a list of ways of ensuring individual accountability in cooperatively structured lessons.

2. Discussing how well the lesson they taught went, identifying positive aspects and problems that arose.

3. Discuss the problems and generate a number of solutions that might be implemented. Revise the lesson to solve any problems.

4. Plan for as many of the members as possible to observe each other teach a lesson structured cooperatively during the following week. Make specific contracts as to what the observer should focus on. An outline of the teacher's role in cooperative learning situations may be helpful.

5. Set agenda and menu for the following week.

The sample agenda for the fourth meeting is as follows:

1. Warm up by handing out material on teaching students the social skills they need to work collaboratively.

2. Discuss how well the observations went and what the members observed. The roles for constructive feedback should be reviewed (see Johnson, 1986). The basic components of cooperative learning situations should also be reviewed. Your role is to ensure that all feedback is constructive and helpful.

3. Plan for the next round of observations.

4. Set the agenda and the menu for the next meeting.

These sample agendas are only aimed at outlining what might happen in the initial meetings of the colleagial support groups. You will need to revise these meeting agendas to better meet the needs of your teachers.

Providing Resources and Incentives

Teachers' perceptions of their interdependence may be considerably enhanced if you offer joint incentives for being an effective colleagial support group. A maxim developed within the business/industrial sector of our society states, "If two individuals get paid for working as a pair, it is amazing how much interest they take in helping one another succeed!" Incentives can be classified as tangible, interpersonal, and personal. Some examples of incentives teachers find valuable are:

1. The opportunity to present an inservice session on cooperative learning procedures to the other members of the staff or to the staff of another school.

2. The opportunity to apply for summer salaries to revise curriculum for cooperatively structured lessons.

3. Visible public praise for their efforts in implementing cooperative learning procedures.

4. Written recognition of their efforts which goes into their individual files.

5. The opportunity to observe teachers in other schools implementing cooperative learning procedures.

To be effective, a colleagial support group will need a variety of resources that only supervisors and principals can provide. Needed resources include:

1. Released time during working hours to meet.

2. A small fund for materials and expenses in implementing cooperative learning.

3. Released time to observe each other teach cooperative lessons.

4. Released time to visit the classrooms of teachers in other schools who are experienced in using cooperative learning procedures.

5. Materials on cooperative learning, such as research updates, helpful hints, sample lesson plans, books, and so forth.

6. Time and resources to help them get started and to help them maintain high interest and involvement in implementing cooperative learning procedures in their classrooms.

7. Emotional support and encouragement to continue their efforts. Always remember that pressure (however subtle) on teachers to implement cooperative learning procedures in their classrooms must be coupled with tangible and visible support from you.

Observe Frequently

Leaders spend their time "where the action is." This means getting out of your office and into classrooms. This visible leadership is called "management by walking around" (Peters & Waterman, 1982). Leaders should visit classrooms frequently, observing instruction in action. Members of colleagial support groups should visit each other's classes frequently, observing cooperative learning in action. The visits do not always have to be long. Besides the structured reciprocal observations members should engage in drop-ins. A **drop-in** is simply an unannounced visit in a clasroom to spend a few minutes observing. The observer may jot down a few notes to highlight something positive observed and then give it to the teacher as a form of feedback during the next colleagial support group meeting.

Celebrating Successes

An essential aspect of providing leadership to colleagial support groups is to observe members using cooperative learning frequently enough that their successes can be celebrated. **A sense of accomplishment complements a sense of purpose.** Both must be nurtured. There is a tremendous power in regular and positive peer feedback. Colleagial support groups need to be designed to produce lots of success in implementing cooperative groups and celebrate it when it occurs. Make use of nonmonetary, interpersonal incentives. Emphasize interpersonal recognition rather than formal evaluation. In essence:

1. Seek out successful implementations of cooperative learning and honor them with all sorts of positive recognition and reinforcement.

2. Seek out opportunities for "good news" swapping among colleagues. Peer respect and recognition are powerful motivators.

In recognizing and celebrating the success of colleagial support group members in implementing cooperative learning, there are a set of errors that may be made and a set of accuracies.

There is nothing more motivating than having colleagues cheering one on and jointly celebrating one's successes. The more effective the school, the more positive peer confirmation is utilized. Create some hoopla within your colleagial support groups and school. Celebrate often!

Discussing How Well the Colleagial Support Groups Function

One area in which most teacher colleagial support groups need considerable help and encouragement is in discussing how well

Table 6.2

Recognizing And Celebrating Cooperative Learning Successes

Errors	Accuracies
Implementation is a mystery.	Implementation is visible.
Tell the principal.	"Good news" swapped among colleagues.
Recognition from principal only.	Peer respect and recognition.
Top few superstars.	Recognition of almost everyone.
Reward for anything.	Valuable action must be completed.

their meetings are contributing to achieving the group's goals and to maintaining effective working relationships among members. This means that you will need to take some initiative in ensuring that one teacher periodically systematically observes a meeting and time is spent on processing how well the group is functioning. After the teachers become experienced in helping their student groups discuss their group functioning, the teachers' abilities to discuss the functioning of their own meetings should increase. But even the most experienced teachers may avoid discussing the functioning of meetings unless the supervisors or principals structure it.

Building Yourself In As a Member

You should be part of each colleagial support group in your jurisdiction. Build yourself in not out! Do not be lonely! Members of a colleagial support group will enjoy considerable success, feel a sense of accomplishment, like each other, see each other as supportive and accepting, and have a sense of camaraderie that significantly increases the quality of their colleagial lives. You should be part of these feelings!

Protecting and Nurturing

When teachers become serious about implementing cooperative learning procedures in their classrooms supervisors and principals will have to do a number of things to protect and nurture the teachers' efforts. Some examples are:

1. There will inevitably be initial failures and problems. Students may be unhappy about the change in the "system," students will be unskilled in working collaboratively, materials may be inappropriate, and what a teacher may define as cooperative learning may not be what you define as cooperative learning. You will have to allow for these initial problems and communicate strongly to your teachers that such initial "start-up costs" are to be expected and accepted. Do not require your teachers to be perfect during the first week they try structuring lessons cooperatively!

2. There will be other innovations within your jurisdiction that will compete for teachers' attention and energy. Part of your responsibilities are to find commonalties of interest and intent among presumably opposing innovations. Encourage your teachers to integrate cooperative learning with other instructional strategies they use or are trying out. But at all costs avoid the cycle of making cooperative learning the focus for a few months or a year and then springing another innovation on your teachers. The "try it and then drop it for the next fad" cycle is especially destructive to quality teaching. Make sure that your teachers recognize that your and their commitment to cooperative learning has to span a number of years.

3. Translate what cooperative learning is so that diverse groups of teachers can understand its importance and usefulness.

4. Deflect, soften, and negate resistance to implementing cooperative learning within your staff. If some teachers believe "I tried that once and it did not work," protect the teachers who are willing to become involved in implementing cooperative learning in their classrooms from demoralizing conversations and criticism from such colleagues.

5. Within any staff there may be destructive competition among teachers as to who is best. Part of your responsibilities are to defuse such "win-lose" dynamics and encourage mutual respect, support, and assistance among your teachers.

6. Within any colleagial support group there will come a time when one member has hurt the feelings of another member or when conflicts arise that disrupt the cohesiveness and productivity of the group. Your task at that point is to ensure that hurt feelings become repaired and that conflicts are constructively resolved. For specific procedures for doing so, see Johnson and Johnson (1987c).

7. Most teachers are concerned that, if a parent complains about their use of cooperative learning procedures, they will receive strong support from their principal and supervisors. Give it. If the parents of the students are concerned and involved in their children's education, they may be curious or even skeptical at any modification of teaching procedures. Be ready to explain why a teacher is using cooperative learning procedures and that it is with your full support and approval.

8. Have the courage to see your teachers through the process of learning how to use cooperative learning procedures effectively.

Think Developmentally

Mastering cooperative learning procedures so that they are used routinely takes time. For most teachers it does not happen in a few weeks or even in a few months. Most teachers work hard for two to three years gaining a thorough understanding of cooperative learning and a solid expertise in using it. You should always think in terms of development, not in radically changing everything the teacher is doing immediately. Have the teacher start with one area, perfect his or her procedures for implementing cooperative learning, and then expand to a second area. Plan developmentally for a two or three year process with heavy emphasis on supporting and maintaining interest. While doing so, you will need to communicate to other staff members that cooperative learning is not this year's fad. A long-term, multi-year emphasis on implementing cooperative learning is required and leaders must protect implementation efforts from being deemphasized to make way for new fads.

Be Inclusive, Not Exclusive

As your success in reaching out to and working with teachers is recognized, teachers will begin asking you to work with them next. Be open to such invitations. When you do not have time to meet all the requests, pair each new teacher with an experienced veteran whom you have trained. Keep your colleagial support groups small. Each time a teacher you are working with achieves some expertise in implementing cooperative learning, pair him or her with a teacher just expressing an interest in doing so. This matchmaking will allow the teacher with newly gained expertise to solidify what they have learned by teaching it to another person. Give guidance as to how to reach out effectively. Keep in contact with the teachers you have worked with and regularly provide support and assistance. Finally, periodically lead a celebration of the success they are having in implementing cooperative learning. **Both a sense of purpose and accomplishment should be nurtured among the teachers you train.**

Points To Remember

1. For your teachers to gain sufficient expertise that they can use cooperative learning routinely without considerable thought and planning will take them two to three years.

2. From working with you and from any training programs they participate in, your teachers will need (1) a clear conceptual model of what "good" cooperative learning is and (2) to be empowered and assisted to practice and practice and practice structuring lessons and units cooperatively.

3. One difficulty in convincing teachers to adopt a new instructional practice is in their fears about the responses it will elicit from students. "When students say x, what will I say back?" is a critical barrier. In order to reduce their fears, your teachers will need to see each other (and you) teach. It is through seeing other teachers respond to students' questions and actions that an understanding of how to do so is achieved. Just as ball-players need to see other people play in order to form a frame-of-reference as to how good they are and where they need to improve, teachers need to compare their implementations of cooperative learning with those of others.

4. The more relaxed and playful teachers are in observing each other in guided practice sessions the better, as the same learning mood will transfer to post-training practice.

A District Strategy

General procedures "cooperative learning leaders" may use in institutionalizing cooperative learning within their school district are as follows:

1. Give a general awareness inservice session to an entire school and ask for volunteers to become a school-based colleagial support group to work systematically on improving their skills in using cooperative learning procedures.

2. Give the basic training in cooperative learning, using this book to ensure that all the critical aspects are covered systematically.

3. Work with each teacher individually:

   a. Teach a cooperatively structured lesson in his or her classroom.

   b. Co-plan a cooperatively structured lesson which is then jointly taught.

   c. Co-plan a lesson that the teacher teaches while you observe.

Through repeated classroom visits each teacher should be trained one-on-one. Some basic rules for working with an individual teacher are:

   a. All lessons are prepared together.

   b. The teacher is the expert on his or her classroom while you are the expert on cooperative learning.

   c. When you are in the teacher's classroom, the teacher owns the lesson. It is the teacher's lesson, not yours.

   d. Each time you meet with a teacher have some new helpful strategy, activity, or set of materials that is tailored to the teacher's subject area or to a specific problem student in the teacher's classroom. This builds a personal as well as a colleagial aspect to the help and assistance in implementing cooperative learning procedures.

4. Network the teachers you are training into colleagial support groups. These groups may meet with and without you.

5. As an additional maintenance procedure, each month send out a newsletter on "How to Help Students Work in Groups." The newsletter contains lesson plans and classroom activities that teachers can try out and/or discuss in the meetings of their colleagial support groups.

6. Meet regularly with curriculum directors, talk to parent groups, attend the principals' cabinet meetings, troubleshoot for your teachers, coordinate collaboration among support group members, and generally spend your days in schools and classrooms.

7. Be genuinely enthusiastic about the use of cooperative learning procedures. Build personal and supportive relationships with the teachers you work with, and show ingenuity in discovering ways to help teachers use cooperative learning procedures.

Summary: Colleagial Support Groups

To lead your school you need to challenge the status quo of competitive / individualistic learning and staff relations, inspire a new vision of cooperative learning in the classroom and cooperation among staff members, empower staff members by organizing them into cooperative teams, lead by example by using cooperative strategies and procedures, and encourage staff members to persevere until they have gained considerable expertise in using cooperative learning. The intent of such leadership is to improve the quality of instruction and learning within the school. Empowering teachers to teach better is the number one priority of leadership.

This means that colleagial support groups are the most important staff cooperative team structured within the school. Gaining expertise requires a cooperative context in which colleagues whom one trusts are committed to one's professional growth and willing to provide assistance, support, and encouragement to further it.

Professional competence is not achieved in isolation from one's peers. When teacher colleagial support groups are structured cooperatively (as opposed to competitively or individualistically) to improve the expertise of all members, productivity will tend to increase as members do in fact gain increased expertise, committed and positive relationships will tend to develop among teachers, social support among staff members will tend to increase, and professional self-esteem will tend to be enhanced. These conclusions are supported by at least 133 studies that have been conducted over the past 90 years. These results apply, however, only when the teacher colleagial support groups have carefully structured positive interdependence, face-to-face promotive interaction, personal responsibility, and periodic group processing. In addition, the teachers must possess the required leadership, communication, trust-building, decision-making, and conflict-management skills.

Colleagial support groups need to be safe places where:

1. Members like to be.

2. There is support, caring, concern, laughter, and camaraderie.

3. The primary goal of improving each other's expertise in implementing cooperative learning is never obscured.

Teacher colleagial support groups cannot survive in isolation. If the classroom and the overall district are structured competitively, the cooperation among teachers needed for teachers to learn from each other will not be sustained. A consistent and coherent organizational structure is established when teachers use cooperative learning in the classroom, administrators organize their faculty into colleagial support groups, and the superintendent organizes the district's administrators into colleagial support groups. The long-term support and assistance necessary for teachers to learn from each other over their entire careers may then be sustained.

Chapter 7

Structuring Schoolwide Task Forces

Empowering Teachers Through Schoolwide Task Forces

Together we stand, divided we fall.

Watchword Of The American Revolution

One day, when the authors were small boys, David tried to lift a heavy stone, but could not budge it. Roger, watching, finally said, "Are you sure you are using **all** your strength? "Yes, I am!" David cried. "No, you're not," said Roger. "You haven't asked me to help you." Within your school and classroom, there are many things you can do by yourself. There are also many things for which you have to use all your strength. When asked to stop students from throwing food on the lunchroom floor, writing on bathroom walls, shoving and pushing other students on the playground and buses, smoking on school property, vandalism, and teasing academically "slower" students before and after school, you are helpless without the support and assistance of your colleagues. It takes the coordinated and committed efforts of all staff members to address such problems. Any one staff member is helpless.

Some decisions administrators or governing councils can make on their own. Other decisions may be made in faculty meetings after a few minutes of discussion. There are decisions, however, that require longer analysis and study before a recommendation may be formulated. A number of schoolwide issues call for assessment and planning. The curriculum in each subject area has to be periodically reviewed and updated. Revision of the curriculum, bus schedules, playground duty, drug use by students, behavior in hallways and lunchroom, a safe and secure school environment, school-parent communications, and many other issues require considered planning and action by the school staff. The responsibility for considering the problem and planning the actions faculty need to take to solve it is given to a schoolwide task force. It is the second type of cooperative team that administrators and governing councils need to structure. You, the leader, organize a faculty task force, negotiate its goals and schedule, and then provide the resources required for the group to function. Membership is not strictly voluntary as sometimes teachers are asked and expected to serve.

Teachers are empowered to solve schoolwide problems when they are placed into schoolwide task forces. **Task forces** plan, recommend, and implement solutions to schoolwide issues and problems. **School task forces** are small problem-solving groups that:

1. Define a problem or issue.

2. Gather data about the nature, causes, and extent of the problem or issue.

3. Consider a variety of alternative actions and solutions.

4. Make conclusions and summarize them into a recommendation.

5. Present and advocate the recommendation to the faculty as a whole.

6. Oversee implementation after the faculty decides whether to accept or modify the task force's recommendations.

To be effective, a schoolwide task force requires:

1. Valid and complete information about the problem or issue.

2. Enough intellectual conflict and disagreement to ensure that all potential solutions get a fair hearing.

3. A method of analysis and synthesis that generates ideas for solutions.

4. Free and informed choice.

5. Continuing motivation to solve the problem if the plan implemented does not work.

In an urban school the authors have recently worked with, for example, a number of students were injured from a variety of causes. One injury resulted from broken playground equipment, two injuries were caused by other students, and two others were just "accidents" that took place in the lunchroom and hallway. The principal became concerned about the increase in students being injured and set up a school task force to consider the issue of reducing student injuries. Three teachers, a counselor, and an assistant principal were asked to serve on the task force. The task force is expected to:

1. **Establish a cooperative structure.** Members must clearly perceive that they "sink or swim together," need to discuss the problem until all members understand its nature and magnitude, are personally accountable for completing their share of the work, need to engage in the social skills required for productive group problem solving, and periodically process how effectively the task force is working.

2. **Identify and define the problem or issue**, that is, determine what a "safety hazard" was and what the school's responsibilities were for preventing accidental injuries. Their definition of the problem included "rough-housing," physical fights and intimidation among the students, students having no place or means to burn off excess physical energy, physical intimidation of faculty and staff by students, safety hazards within the building and playground, and any other factors that the task force determined to be potential causes of injuries.

3. **Gather information about the existence of safety issues within the school.** Once the issue was defined, the task force gathered data on how many hazards actually existed, how much of a danger they actually were, and how frequently certain student behaviors occurred. Once the safety and behavioral issues were defined and their existence documented, the task force analyzed the causes and determinants of each issue.

4. **Identify potential solutions to each issue.** A number of potential solutions were identified for each safety hazard. The cost of having regular inspections made of playground equipment and lunchroom tables, for example, was assessed. Supervised activities in the gym and playground were considered.

5. **Decide on which solutions to recommend to the faculty to adopt.** Out of the wide range of potential solutions identified, several were chosen to be included in the recommendation to be made to the faculty as a whole.

6. **Make a 20 minute presentation of the recommendations during a staff meeting.** When the task force was ready, they made a 20 minute presentation summarizing their work and their recommendation was made during a faculty meeting. They summarized their procedures and the range of options considered, and then advocated their recommendation as the best set of actions available. The

presentation was aimed at being as persuasive as possible and a variety of charts, graphs, and diagrams were used. The recommendation included measurable objectives, the key steps for achieving each objective, the factors that were anticipated as blocking or facilitating solutions, time lines, responsibilities, and ways to evaluate the results if the recommendations were adopted by the faculty.

7. **Deciding as an entire staff as to whether or not the recommendations should be adopted.** Because the issue seemed complex, the principal decided to delay the decision to accept or modify the recommendations until the next faculty meeting. During the subsequent faculty meeting the principal assigned faculty members to triads, each triad made a decision as to whether to accept or modify the task force's recommendations, each triad made a brief report of their reasoning to the faculty as a whole, a short discussion was held in the faculty meeting, and then a formal decision was made by the entire staff. This use of ad hoc decision-making groups is discussed in the next chapter.

8. **Evaluating extent of implementation and its success.** The responsibilities of the task force do not end when the faculty makes a decision to adopt their recommendation (perhaps after modifying it in some way). The plan has to be implemented. The task force documents the extent to which implementation takes place, notes barriers to implementation, and evaluates the success of the plan in reducing student injuries. If the plan does not reduce the frequency of student injuries, then the task force must repeat the problem-solving process and come up with another recommendation for the faculty to consider.

A schoolwide task force may be set up by the building administration, by a governing council made up of faculty members, or by a combination of the two. Whoever commissions the task force is responsible for ensuring that the above steps are followed when schoolwide issues and problems need to be dealt with by the faculty. Each of the eight steps is discussed below.

Establishing A Cooperative Structure

In a school cafeteria a teacher was trying to hang a four-by-eight-foot banner on the wall. Another teacher saw him struggling and walked over and offered to assist. "No," the first teacher replied, "I can do it myself." After much solitary effort, the banner was in place and proudly proclaimed the message: "Together, we can find the answers."

There are a number of classic errors that administrators and governing councils make in creating task forces within a school. The **first** and most severe is assuming that staff members will work cooperatively if they are told to serve on a task force and placed in the same room. Task forces may be characterized by competition and power conflicts among members or they may function more like "individualistic efforts with talking" than a cooperative effort. If you want staff members to work together productively, a clear cooperative structure must be established. The **second** fallacious assumption is that staff members have the leadership, decision-making, trust-building, communication, and conflict-management skills they need to work together effectively. Neither assumption is justified in most schools. Adults in our society typically do not have the small group and interpersonal skills to work cooperatively and even when they do they often do not use their skills because the situation is not clearly structured cooperatively.

What often happens in task forces is lack of involvement and commitment by members with the official chairperson being responsible for doing all the work. Members can adopt a "leave it to George" attitude and expend decreasing amounts of effort and just go through the team-work motions. At the same time George may expend less effort in order to avoid the "sucker effect" of doing all the work. The responsibility to come up with innovative ideas can become so diffused that no one feels accountable. Conflicts among members may be managed destructively, causing members to become alienated from the task and each other. All the potential problems with small group work may be avoided by ensuring cooperation is carefully and clearly structured.

A schoolwide task force is first and foremost a cooperative team. Like all cooperative teams, five basic elements need to be carefully structured:

1. **Positive interdependence**: Members must perceive that they sink or swim together. The goal of the task force is to come to a joint conclusion as to what course of action will best solve a schoolwide problem. Decisions should be made by consensus with all members of the group being convinced that the recommended actions are the most promising. Members must challenge the status quo of dealing with the problem and create a vision of alternative and more effective solutions.

2. **Face-to-face promotive interaction**: Members must discuss the issue thoroughly face-to-face. Creative insight and higher-level reasoning about the problem comes from face-to-face discussions in which members explain their ideas and the rationale behind their conclusions. Members are responsible for not only commit ting themselves the group effort, but also promoting the success and contributions of all other members. Task force members must have confidence in the ability of the group to solve the problem, be supportive of other group members, confirm and recognize the valuable contributions others make to the group's efforts, and believe that their central abilities are being utilized and valued by the group.

3. **Individual accountability**: Each member must feel personally responsible and accountable for contributing his or

her fair share of the work. Clear assistance should be given to each member with members holding each other accountable to come to meetings prepared.

4. **Social skills**: Members must provide the leadership, communication, trust-building, decision-making, conflict-management, and other cooperative skills required to function effectively.

5. **Group processing**: Members must process how effectively they are working together. This requires structured discussions of how well the group is functioning and an analysis of how the interaction among group members can become more productive.

These five basic elements are as essential for staff task forces as they are for cooperative learning groups. After forming a task force and explaining the problem to be solved, the convener clearly establishes that the members "sink or swim together," must engage in considerable face-to-face discussion of the problem, are individually accountable for completing their share of the group's work, are responsible for being a skillful and constructive member, and must periodically process how effectively the task force is working. The behavioral expectations for each member and the criterion for success should be clear.

Identifying And Defining The Problem Or Issue

Once upon a time, a young rabbit decided to go out into the world and seek his fortune. His parents gave him $500, wished him well, and he began his search. Before he had traveled very far he met a pack rat.

"Hey, little rabbit, where are you going?" asked the pack rat.

"I'm seeking my fortune," replied the young rabbit.

"You're in luck," said the pack rat. *"I have here a suit of beautiful clothes that I will sell to you for only $100. Then you can go seeking your fortune looking prosperous and stylish!"*

"Say, that's fantastic!" replied the young rabbit, who immediately brought the clothes, put them on, and continued his search for his fortune. Soon he met a deer.

"Hey, little rabbit, where are you going?" asked the deer.

"I'm seeking my fortune," replied the young rabbit.

"You're in great luck," said the deer. *"For only $300, I will sell you this motorcycle so you can go seeking your fortune at great and exciting speeds!"*

"Say, that's fantastic!" replied the young rabbit, who immediately bought the motorcycle and went zooming across the countryside. Soon he met a coyote.

"Hey, little rabbit, where are you going?" asked the coyote.

"I'm seeking my fortune," replied the young rabbit.

"You're in great luck!" said the coyote. *"For a measly $100 , I will let you take a shortcut,"* said the coyote, pointing to his open mouth, *"and you will save yourself years of time!"*

"Say, that's fantastic!" replied the young rabbit. And paying his last $100 he put his head into the coyote's mouth, and was immediately devoured.

The moral of this story is: If you don't know where you are going, you are likely to end up somewhere you do not want to be!

The first step of the task force is to identify and define the problem. A **problem** may be defined as a discrepancy or difference between an actual state of affairs and a desired state of affairs. Problem solving requires both an idea about where the school should be and valid information about where it is now. The more clear and accurate the definition of the problem, the easier it is to do the other steps in the problem-solving processes. The school vision, mission, and goals are relevant to defining the problem. There are three steps in defining the problem:

1. Reaching agreement on what the desired state of affairs is.

2. Obtaining valid, reliable, directly verifiable, descriptive (not inferential or evaluative), and correct information about the existing state of affairs.

3. Discussing thoroughly the difference between the desired and actual state of affairs, because it is from the awareness of this discrepancy that the commitment and motivation to solve the problem is built.

Because problem-solving groups often progress too quickly toward a solution to the problem without first getting a clear, consensual definition of the problem itself, members of the group should see to it that everyone understands what the problem is before trying to assess its magnitude.

Defining a workable problem is often the hardest stage of the problem-solving process. Suggestions for procedures are as follows:

1. List a series of statements about the problem. Describe it as concretely as possible by mentioning people, places, and resources. There should be as many different statements of the problem as the members are willing to give. Write them on a blackboard where everyone can see them. Avoid arguing about whether the problem is perfectly stated.

2. Restate each problem statement so that is includes a description of both the desired and actual state of affairs.

Take out alternative definitions that are beyond the resources of the group to solve. Choose the definition that the group members agree is most correct. **The problem should be important, solvable, and urgent.**

3. Write out a detailed description of what school life will be like when the problem is solved. The more detailed and specific the scenario is, the better.

There are a number of potential barriers to identifying and defining problems. The first is **prematurely defining the problem**. The direction a group first takes in defining the problem may keep it from finding a successful solution (Maier, 1930); therefore, the group should be careful not to agree prematurely on the definition of its problem. The second is a **lack of clarity in stating the problem**. Much of the initial effort of groups in solving a problem is directed toward orienting members to what the problem is. This phase is extremely important, and it deserves sufficient time and effort to identify the problem, to define it, and, through this process, to get the members involved in and committed to solving it. Often, groups are doomed to failure when they inadequately define the nature of their problem. Third, **a critical, evaluative, competitive climate** prevents creative and workable solutions from being discovered. A supportive, trusting, cooperative atmosphere is necessary for solving problems successfully. If group members are afraid that other members are evaluating their ideas, effective problem solving is destroyed. Fourth, if group members have **inadequate motivation to solve the problem** a compelling solution will not be found. Any problem-solving group must have the motivation to solve its problems. If the group members are not motivated, they must be persuaded to see the importance of the problem and the necessity for seeking a solution. Members who leave the work to others clearly lack motivation.

Gathering Information About The Existence Of The Problem

The second step in the problem-solving process is diagnosing the existence, magnitude, and nature of the problem. Valid information must be gathered. Then the information must be thoroughly discussed and analyzed to ensure that all task force members understand it. Actual frequency of occurrence of the problem, the magnitude of the forces helping the school to move toward the desired state of affairs, and the forces hindering this movement need to be documented. Determining what forces are acting upon the problem situation is called **force field analysis** (Lewin, 1945; Myrdal, 1944). In force field analysis the problem is seen as a balance between forces working in opposite directions--some helping the movement toward the desired state of affairs and others restraining such movement. The balance that results between the helping and restraining forces is the actual state of affairs--a **quasi-stationary equilibrium** that can be altered through changes in the forces.

FIGURE 7.1   Force Field Analysis

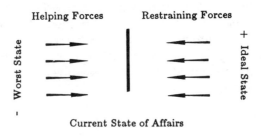

The ideal state of affairs toward which the group is working is on the right side and is represented by a plus sign. The worst state of affairs, on the left side of the figure, is represented by a minus sign. The vertical line in the middle signifies the current state of affairs--a middle ground. On any problem numerous forces are at work, some restraining change and others helping change. There are two basic steps for a group to follow in doing a force field analysis:

1. Make up lists of forces by first brainstorming all the helping forces and then all the restraining forces. The list should include all possible forces, whether psychological, interpersonal, organizational, or societal. If a force seems to be a complex of variables, each variable should be listed separately. Critical judgment should be avoided; it is essential that every member's ideas are publicly requested and aired.

2. Rank the forces according to their importance in affecting the present situation. Agree on the most important helping and restraining forces, which may total from three to six each. Rate the important forces according to how easily they can be resolved, and avoid spending time discussing those that the group cannot influence with their current resources.

An example is as follows. The implementation of cooperative learning within a school may be seen as a balance between forces helping teachers implement cooperative learning and restraining teachers from using cooperative learning. The use of cooperative learning is promoted by the teachers' awareness that it will increase student achievement, higher-level reasoning, social skills, self-esteem, and social support. The use of cooperative learning is restrained by teachers habitually using other instructional procedures, not being willing to commit the time to learn how to use cooperative learning, inherent fear of change, lack of willingness to revise their standard lessons, and incomplete understanding of what cooperative learning is.

FIGURE 7.2 Implementing Cooperative Learning

HELPING FORCES   RESTRAINING FORCES

No Use −   + Skilled Use

Achievement increases ►	◄ Habit of status quo
Higher level reasoning ►	◄ Time needed to learn how
Improved social skills ►	◄ Fear of change
Increased self-esteem ►	◄ Time to revise lessons
More social support ►	◄ Lack of understanding
Liking for school ►	◄ Teacher isolation

Current Level of Use

There are two major **barriers** to gathering valid information about the nature and magnitude of the problem. The first is **not getting the needed information.** When information is minimal, the definition of the problem will be inadequate, fewer alternative strategies for the solution will be generated, and potential consequences of those alternatives will not be properly explored. The result is relatively low-grade solutions. Great emphasis must be placed on fact finding in order to solve a problem effectively. The second barrier is **poor communication within the group.** Poor communication among group members has the same effect as the lack of information, with the added problem that it makes the implementation of any action that requires coordination among group members difficult. Effective communication among all group members is necessary for effective problem solving.

Without defining the problem correctly and specifically, it cannot be adequately understood. And without an accurate and precise understanding of the forces involved, the alternative strategies for the solution of the problem cannot be formulated.

Formulating And Considering Alternative Solutions

The overall purpose of a schoolwide task force is to provide the staff with a free and informed choice of a solution to the problem based on having and understanding the relevant information. To achieve that purpose a cooperative structure must be established within the task force, the problem must be accurately identified and defined, and valid information about the existence, magnitude, and nature of the problem must be gathered and organized so it is easily understood. Once the nature and magnitude of the problem is accurately understood, alternative ways to solve it may be identified.

The fourth step in task force problem solving is identifying and analyzing alternative ways to solve the problem. Groups often make poor decisions because they (a) do not think of the proper alternative solutions and/or (b) do a poor job of evaluating and choosing among the alternatives considered. **Systematically evaluating each alternative and analyzing the advantages and disadvantages of each alternative before making a final decision are the most important factors in effective decision making.** The more explicit the systematic evaluation the less likely that an alternative will be overlooked or rationalized away. If decision makers do know what the alternatives are and have correctly diagnosed each alternative's inherent advantages and disadvantages, they will not choose a certain course of action unless its advantages are expected to exceed its disadvantages.

Identifying and analyzing alternative ways to solve the problem requires creative, divergent, and inventive reasoning. Such "higher-level" thinking and analysis comes primarily from intellectual disagreement and challenge, i.e., controversy. **Controversy** exists when one member's ideas, information, conclusions, theories, or opinions are incompatible with those of another member and the two seek to reach agreement (Johnson & Johnson, 1979, 1987b). In contrast to controversy, **concurrence seeking** occurs when members inhibit discussion to avoid any disagreement and emphasize agreement. There is considerable evidence that structured controversy, through the use of advocacy subgroups, promotes greater understanding and long-term retention of the information being discussed, higher quality and more creative decision making, and higher level reasoning than does concurrence seeking, debate, or individual decision-making (Johnson & F. Johnson, 1987; Johnson & R. Johnson, 1979, 1987; Johnson, John son, Smith, & Tjosvold, 1989; Johnson & Tjosvold, 1983). In addition, controversy promotes more positive relationships among group members, greater perceived colleagial support, higher self-esteem, and greater social skills. By definition, all decisions involve controversy as **decision making** is a process that results in a choice among alternative courses of action. Controversy is structured within problem-solving groups through the use of advocacy subgroups.

Advocacy Subgroups

> *Since the general or prevailing opinion on any subject is rarely or never the whole truth, it is only by the collision of adverse opinion that the remainder of the truth has any chance of being supplied.*

John Stuart Mill

The president of a large pharmaceutical company, faced with a decision of whether to buy or build a chemical plant, established two advocacy groups (**The Wall Street Journal**, October 22, 1975). The "buy" team was instructed to present the best case for purchasing a chemical plant, and the "build" team was told to present the best case for constructing a new chemical plant near the company's national headquarters. The "buy" team identified over 100 existing plants that would meet the company's needs, narrowed the field down to 20, further narrowed the field down to 3, and then selected 1 plant as the ideal plant to buy. The "build" team contacted dozens of engineering firms and, after four months of consideration, selected a design for the ideal plant to build. The two teams, armed with all the details about cost, presented their best case to the company's management team. From the presentations, it was apparent that the two options would cost about the same amount of money and, therefore, the team selected the "build" option because it allowed the plant to be conveniently located near company headquarters.

Advocacy subgroups are created when a number of alternative solutions are being considered and the task force wants to ensure that each gets a fair and complete hearing. Each advocacy subgroup prepares and presents a particular policy alternative to the task force. The procedure for using advocacy subgroups is:

1. Identify the alternative solutions to the problem.

2. Assign members to advocacy subgroups.

3. Give advocacy subgroups time to prepare their position and supporting rationale. Members organize available information to support their position.

4. Have each subgroup present and elaborate their position and rationale to the task force.

5. Have an open discussion in which subgroups argue their points-of-view and refute the other positions. Each position should be critically evaluated with doubts and objections freely expressed. In effect, each subgroup is a **devil's advocate** in criticizing the other positions.

6. Have each subgroup present the opposing positions. This perspective-reversal ensures that each subgroup listens carefully to the other presentations and comprehends their rationales completely.

7. Synthesize the best arguments from all sides and synthesize until a consensus is reached. A report is then written and a presentation to the entire faculty is planned.

In order to participate competently in the controversy process staff members must be able to prepare a position, advocate it, defend it from criticism, critically evaluate the alternative positions, be able to view the problem from all perspectives, and be able to synthesize and integrate the best parts of all solutions.

Force-Field Analysis

The use of advocacy subgroups ensures that controversy is managed constructively within the task force and that all perspectives are considered. During the analysis and synthesis of the alternative solutions a method is needed.

Force field analysis is a particularly useful way of specifying alternative strategies for solving a problem. It is based on the assumption that changes in the present situation will occur only as the helpful and restraining forces are changed so that the level where they are balancing is altered. **There are two basic methods for changing the equilibrium point between the two sets of forces**: increasing the strength or number of the helping forces and decreasing the strength or number of the restraining forces.

Of the two, the preferable strategy is to reduce the strength or eliminate the restraining forces. Increasing the pressure for change in the present situation by strengthening the helping forces also increases natural resistances to change, reducing the strategy's effectiveness. Restraining forces may be reduced or eliminated without creating resistance. **Reducing the restraining forces, therefore, is usually the more effective of the two strategies.** The fewer the forces acting upon the present situation, furthermore, the lower the tension level of the people in the situation.

The two strategies are not mutually exclusive. Often you will wish to reduce restraining forces and increase helping forces at the same time. When this can be done, it is very effective. One way of intervening simultaneously with both types of forces is to modify a restraining force so that it becomes a helping force.

Returning to the example of using cooperative learning, if teachers are ordered to use cooperative learning procedures to increase student achievement, they naturally resist and undermine any efforts to make them do so. If teachers interested in implementing cooperative learning are organized into colleagial support groups, their isolation is reversed, their fear of change and dependence on the status quo is reduced by the social support they receive, and the assistance they receive reduces the time required for planning cooperative lessons.

One of the most successful strategies for changing the direction of a restraining force is to involve the group members who are resisting the desired changes in diagnosing the problem situation and in planning the solutions (Watson & Johnson, 1972). **People enjoy and affirm the changes they make themselves, and they resist changes imposed upon them by others.** Involvement of resisters in the diagnosing and planning of change often means a more difficult planning process, but it virtually guarantees that they are committed to the proposed changes. It also helps clear up any misunderstandings and differences of opinion before the strategies are implemented, and it uses the resources of the "opposition."

Force field analysis is useful for two reasons. First, it avoids the error of a single-factor analysis of a problem; using it will keep attention on the problem situation until a number of relevant factors are identified. **Second**, by helping to identify a number of problem-related factors, it gives group members several points at which they may intervene in their attempt to produce a change. Because any change is the result of a number of factors, an effective change strategy involves plural actions that are directed toward several of those factors. When an approach is made through modifying several factors at the same time, the possibility is increased that the improvement will be permanent.

In specifying alternative strategies for change, group members should think of as many ways as possible in which the forces holding the group from moving toward the desired state might be reduced. They should obtain ideas from everyone in the group. If group members do not have many ideas, outside consultants can always be invited to lend assistance. Bringing in an expert who knows a lot about the substance of the problem is often extremely helpful at this point. Group members should try to take each restraining force in turn and think up ways to reduce its strength or to eliminate it altogether. Divergent thinking should be encouraged.

Vigilant Analysis

Janis and Mann (1977) recommend a procedure they believe eliminates the possibility of defensive avoidance and ensures that vigilant consideration of each alternative solution takes place. The task force systematically evaluates each alternative solution on the basis of four factors:

1. The tangible gains and losses for the school staff.

2. The tangible gains and losses for significant others such as parents and other members of the school district.

3. Staff self-approval or self-disapproval (*Will we feel proud or ashamed if we choose this alternative?*).

4. The approval or disapproval of the school by significant others (*Will important people we are connected with think we made the right decision?*).

The task force ensures that these four factors are used to analyze each alternative by:

1. A balance sheet is completed for each course of action considered. A balance sheet consists of listing the tangible gains from adopting the alternative on one side and the tangible losses on the other.

2. Each gain or loss is rated in terms of its importance on a ten-point scale from "1" (no importance) to "10" (extremely important).

3. After a balance sheet is completed for each alternative course of action, the balance sheets are compared and the alternatives are ranked from "most desirable" to "least desirable."

Using a balance sheet to ensure systematic evaluation has been found to be related to level of satisfaction with a decision, commitment to a decision, and security about the correctness of a decision (Janis & Mann, 1977).

Barriers

There are a number of barriers to formulating and considering alternative solutions to the problem. The first is a **failure to identify the proper alternative courses of action**. If a course of action is not identified, it cannot be considered and evaluated. The second is **premature elimination of courses of action without proper analysis and evaluation, or uninformed and premature choice.** For most people, ideas are fragile creations, easily blighted by a chill, or even indifferent, reception. As groups proceed in their problem-solving activities, they must avoid all tendencies to squelch each idea as it comes along; instead, they should create an atmosphere that supports the presentation and the pooling of a wide assortment of ideas. All alternative solutions should receive a fair hearing. Only then can the group avoid becoming fixated on the first reasonable solution suggested and critically evaluate the worth of all alternatives. The third is **pressures for conformity.** Pressures for conformity and compliance slow down the development of different and diverse ideas. Divergent thinking as well as convergent thinking are necessary for sound problem solving. The fourth is **a lack of inquiry and problem-solving skills.** Some groups may need special training in how to use inquiry and problem-solving methods to advantage. Training may be accomplished through an expert member of the group, or the group may wish to call in an outside consultant. The fifth is **a lack of procedures to aid analysis and synthesis.** The forces creating the problem must be understood and systematically analyzed in order for new alternatives to be created.

Deciding On A Solution

Once all the possible solutions have been identified and formulated in specific terms, the group needs to select the solution it will implement. Making a decision involves considering possible alternatives and choosing one. The purpose of group decision making is to decide on well-considered, well-understood, realistic action toward goals every member wishes to achieve. A **decision** implies that some agreement prevails among group members as to which of several courses of action is most desirable for achieving the group's goals. **Decision making** is a process that results in a choice among alternative courses of action. There are five major characteristics of an effective decision (Johnson & F. Johnson, 1987):

1. The resources of group members are fully utilized.

2. Time is well used.

3. The decision is correct or of high quality. A **high quality decision** solves the problem, can be implemented in a way that the problem does not reoccur, and does **not** require more time, people, and material resources than the school can provide.

4. All the required staff members are fully committed to implementing the decision.

5. The problem-solving ability of the group is enhanced, or at least not lessened.

Decision By Consensus

There are many methods, such as decision by majority vote or by the person with the most authority, for making decisions. Whenever possible, decisions by task forces should be made by consensus. Consensus is the most effective method of group decision making, but it also takes the most time. Perfect consensus means that everyone agrees what the decision should be. Unanimity, however, is often impossible to achieve. There are degrees of consensus, all of which bring about a higher-quality decision than majority vote or other methods of decision making. **Consensus** is more commonly defined as a collective opinion arrived at by a group of individuals working together under conditions that permit communications to be sufficiently open and the group climate to be sufficiently supportive for everyone in the group to feel that he or she has had a fair chance to influence the decision. When a decision is made by consensus, all members understand the decision and are prepared to support it. In operation, consensus means that all members can rephrase the decision to show that they understand it, that all members have had a chance to tell the group how they feel about the decision, and that those members who continue to disagree or have doubts will nevertheless say publicly that they are willing to give the decision a try for a period of time.

To achieve consensus, members must have enough time to state their views and, in particular, their opposition to other members' views. By the time the decision is made they should be feeling that others really do understand them. Group members, therefore, must listen carefully and communicate effectively. Decisions made by consensus are sometimes referred to as synergistic decisions, because the group members working together arrive at a decision of higher quality than the decision they would obtain if each one worked separately. In reaching consensus, group members need to see differences of opinion, i.e., controversy, as a way of (1) gathering additional information, (2) clarifying issues, (3) ensuring the group to seeks better alternatives, and (4) seeing the problem from a variety of perspectives.

The basic guidelines for consensual decision making are
as follows:

1. **Avoid arguing blindly for your own opinions.** Present your
   position as clearly and logically as possible, but listen to
   other members' reactions and consider them carefully
   before you press your point.

2. **Avoid changing your mind only to reach agreement and
   avoid conflict.** Support only solutions with which you are
   at least somewhat able to agree. Yield only to positions that
   have objective and logically sound foundations.

3. **Avoid conflict-reducing procedures** such as majority
   voting, tossing a coin, averaging, and bargaining.

4. **Seek out differences of opinion.** They are natural and expected. Try to involve everyone in the decision process.
   Disagreements can improve the group's decision because
   they present a wide range of information and opinions,
   thereby creating a better chance for the group to hit upon
   more adequate solutions.

5. **Do not assume that someone must win and someone
   must lose** when discussion reaches a stalemate. Instead,
   strive for an integration or synthesis that includes the best
   arguments from all sides.

6. **Discuss underlying assumptions and rationales**, listen
   carefully to one another, and encourage the participation
   of all members.

Consensus is the best method for producing an innovative,
creative, and high-quality decision that (1) all members will be committed to implementing, (2) uses the resources of all group members, and (3) increases the future decision-making effectiveness of
the group. Consensus is not easy to achieve as it is characterized
by more conflict among members, more shifts of opinion, a longer
time to reach a conclusion, and more confidence by members in

the correctness of their decision. It is, however, worth the time and trouble.

Second-Chance Meeting

Even when decisions are made by consensus, there are times when members fixate on an alternative without thinking through all its consequences. One procedure for ensuring that a decision is not made too hastily is **second-chance meetings**. Alfred Sloan, when he was Chairman of General Motors, once called an executive meeting to consider a major decision. He concluded the meeting by saying, *"Gentlemen, I take it we are all in complete agreement on the decision here...Then I propose we postpone further discussion until our next meeting to give ourselves time to develop disagreement and perhaps gain some understanding of what the decision is all about."* After a preliminary consensus on the best alternative, a **second-chance meeting** can be held in which all members are encouraged to express any remaining doubts and criticisms. Second chance meetings help prevent premature consensus and concurrence seeking.

There are a number of societies that have assumed that under the influence of alcohol there would be fewer inhibitions against expressing residual doubts about a preliminary decision made when everyone was sober. According to Herodotus, the ancient Persians would make important decisions twice--first sober and then drunk. According to Tacitus, the Germans in Roman times also followed this practice. In Japan, where an emphasis is placed on harmony and politeness, a decision is frequently reconsidered after work in a bar. "Sake talk" takes place after each person has had a couple of cups of sake and, therefore, is no longer required to be polite. How group members really feel about the decision is then revealed.

In vino veritas?

Presenting The Recommendation To The Faculty

It is not enough to make a decision. All staff members who need to implement the decision need to be convinced that it is the best thing to do. Thus, the solution recommended has to be clearly communicated to the staff as a whole and the staff must have an opportunity to modify the decision if they are to be committed to implementing it. During a faculty meeting the task force presents its recommendations by defining the problem, proposing its recommendations, presenting its rationale and reasoning, and making the best and most persuasive case possible for its conclusions. The task force:

1. Presents its solution to the problem.

2. Lists and details the facts, information, and experiences gathered that validate the solution.

3. Links the facts together into a logical structure that leads to the conclusion. The available information may be divided into three parts: most important, moderately important, and least important to the claim being made. The task force should build a coherent position out of isolated facts by putting information together, arranging and composing it, structuring ideas to make their case, and striving for solid evidence and sound reasoning.

If the recommendation is not presented sincerely and forcefully, it will not receive a fair hearing. If the diagnosis and reasoning of the task force is not clear, then the recommendation will not make sense to the rest of the staff.

Having The Faculty Decide

After the recommendation has been presented, the faculty as a whole decides to accept or modify the recommendation. The next chapter deals with this phase of the problem-solving process in detail. If the faculty and staff as a whole are not involved in the making of the decision, they will have little or no commitment to help implement the decision. People tend to affirm, support, and implement decisions they have helped make while they tend to resist implementation of decisions imposed on them. The key to this step is to ensure that everyone participates, every one is involved in making the decision, and, therefore, everyone is committed to implementing the decision once it is made. The **barrier** to effective decision making at this point is inadequate involvement of the individuals who have to implement the decision.

Evaluating Extent And Success Of Implementation

Decision implementation is a process of taking the necessary actions that result in the execution of the decision. **Decision implementation requires internal commitment by relevant staff members to the decisions made.** No decision is worthwhile unless it is implemented. Once the faculty decides, the next step is going out and doing what they have decided to do.

The responsibilities of the task force do not end when the faculty makes a decision to adopt their recommendation (perhaps after modifying it). The plan has to be implemented. The task force documents the extent to which implementation takes place, notes barriers to implementation, and evaluates the success of the plan. If the plan does not succeed, then the task force must repeat the problem-solving process and come up with another recommendation for the faculty to consider.

To evaluate the success of the solution the staff has decided to implement, the task force members must determine (1) whether the solution was successfully implemented and (2) what the effects were. The first activity is sometimes called **process evaluation** because it deals with the process of implementing a strategy. The second is called **outcome evaluation** because it involves assessing or judging the consequences of implementing the strategy. Planners should establish criteria for or ways in which to judge the effectiveness of their actions in implementing the strategy, and review their progress as each action step occurs. The major criterion for assessing the outcome of an implemented strategy is whether the actual state of affairs is closer to the desired state of affairs than it was before the strategy was carried out.

If the group finds that its solution has been successfully implemented, but has failed to change substantially the current situation into the ideal state of affairs, a new solution must be chosen and implemented until the group finds one that is effective. The solution of one set of problems, however, often brings other problems into the open, and in trying out various strategies the group may find that it has not been working for the solution of the most critical problem in the situation. The final result of the evaluation stage, therefore, should be to show the group what problems have been solved and to what extent, what problems still need to be solved, and what new problems have come up. Evaluation should result in a new definition of a problem, a rediagnosis of the situation, and beginning of a new problem-solving sequence.

Summary

Staff members are empowered to solve schoolwide problems when they are organized into task forces and given the charge of formulating a solution that will be presented to the entire faculty for approval or modification. **School task forces** are small problem-solving groups. To be effective they need to collect valid and complete information about the problem, engage in controversy to ensure that all alternative solutions get a fair hearing, synthesize the best points from all perspectives, and make a free and informed choice in a way that creates continuing motivation to solve the problem if the plan does not work. Task forces must establish a cooperative structure, identify and define the problem, gather information about the nature and magnitude of the problem, formulate and consider alternative solutions (utilizing advocacy subgroups to do so), decide on which solution to adopt, present and advocate the solution to the entire staff, and evaluate the extent and success of the implementation.

DOES YOUR TASK FORCE MEASURE UP?

Use the checklist below to see
if you have included
the basic elements in your structure.

☐ Positive Interdependence

☐ Face-to-Face Promotive
   Interaction

☐ Individual Accountability

☐ Social Skills

☐ Group Processing

Chapter 8

Ad Hoc Decision-Making Groups

Empowering Teachers Through Decision-Making Groups

Aesop, in about 550 BC, told the story of the bundle of sticks. A father wearied of his sons quarrelling despite how often he asked them not to. One day when the quarreling was especially devisive, he asked one of his sons to bring him a bundle of sticks. Then handing the bundle to each of his sons in turn, he asked them to try to break it. But although each one tried with all his strength, none was able to do so. The father then untied the bundle and gave the sticks to his sons to break one by one. This they did very easily. *"My sons,"* said the father, *"do you not see how certain it is that if you agree with each other and help each other, it will be impossible for your enemies to injure you? But if you are divided among yourselves, you will be no stronger than a single stick in that bundle."* The moral of the tale is, __in unity is strength__. **Involving all staff members in making the important school decisions is the primary means of obtaining the unity that gives the implemention of the decision strength.**

In the United States, teachers are typically not involved in making school decisions. According to a nationwide poll involving 21,698 teachers conducted by the Carnegie Foundation for the Advancement of Teaching and released in October of 1988, 90 percent of teachers felt left out of critical decisions affecting classroom life such as teacher evaluation and the selection of new teachers and administrators. Twenty-one percent felt left out of decisions choosing textbooks and instructional materials, 37 percent stated they had no say in shaping curriculum, and 55 percent reported having no influence in tracking students into special classes.

The direct involvement of most teachers in making decisions could occur during faculty meetings. In a recent faculty meeting we observed, however, there was general confusion concerning a decision made the week before. No one seemed to remember the decision and, therefore, the decision had not been implemented. Staff members seemed not to care, leaving the problem for the principal to solve. During the meeting there was general inattentiveness with teachers engaging in side conversations, grading papers, knitting, and even reading the newspaper. Many of the agenda items were either greeted with silence or with negative comments about the item or the contributions of colleagues. Occasionally cynical remarks would be volunteered, such as "LMV" (Let's make it voluntary) and "Can we work in our rooms instead?"

Faculty meetings should provide an opportunity for participation and verbal exchange not found in other communication channels, such as memos, newsletters, or announcements on the loud speaker. One-way messages are not effective in many instances. When the input of staff members is desired, when staff members will have to implement the decision, or when the support of staff members is needed, faculty meetings are required. Within a faculty meeting there are **informational** items to which staff members are supposed to listen and retain, **procedural** items to which staff members are supposed to listen and give suggestions if they wish, and **problems** to which alternatives have to be generated and a decision made.

It is not easy to run a good faculty meeting. The secret is using a small-group / larger-group decision-making procedure. There are six major reasons for using such a cooperative procedure within faculty meetings. **The first is to model the use of cooperative procedures to show your support of and emphasis on the use of cooperative learning groups in classrooms.** How the leader runs the faculty meeting is a model for how all staff members should approach their responsibilities. Leaders lead by example. What you do far outweighs what you say. Verbally encouraging teachers to use cooperative learning procedures and then conducting faculty meetings in a direct teaching / lecture manner is a contradiction. All too frequently the leader does most of the talking and staff members are placed in the passive position of listening and commenting. Active, involved, and thoughtful participation in faculty meetings result from cooperative interaction among staff members. Using cooperative procedures in faculty meetings is the strongest recommendation for cooperative teaching an administrator or school leader can make. Faculty meetings are a perfect place to model the use of cooperative strategies and procedures. If you want teachers to use cooperative learning, you have to be willing to use cooperative procedures within faculty meetings.

The second reason for using cooperative procedures within faculty meetings is to to empower staff members. A teacher may not like the lunchroom behavior of students but feel helpless to do anything about it. One teacher may want to stop students from defacing school property, but feel helpless to do anything about it. The watchword of the American Revolution was, **"United we stand, divided we fall!"** Where one teacher is helpless, the coordinated efforts of all staff members is powerful. All staff members working together can change the lunchroom behavior of students and can decrease significantly the defacing of school property by students. Staff members are empowered when they are placed in cooperative teams and given the responsibility to solve schoolwide problems. All staff members then share the responsibility for implementing the decisions made and are more motivated to do so.

The third reason is to moderize the school as an organization. In the business world, most of the important work is done by groups rather than individuals. For example, the development of most computer systems requires highly interactive groups of knowledgeable workers. Similarly, the number of people coauthoring scientific papers has increased dramatically in recent years. In 1986, 75 people co-authored a paper with evidence related to the location of the gene for Duchenne muscular dystrophy. Having teachers work in cooperative teams and thereby involving them in the making of important school decisions is one way to "modernize" the school.

The fourth reason for using cooperative procedures is to improve the quality of the decision. High involvement in decision making increases the use of the members' resources, which in turn increases the quality of the decision. No single person in an organization can expect to have all the information necessary to make a decision. Most decisions must be handled by groups because each individual will have only a certain amount of the information necessary to make a valid decision. As a result, the accuracy of the information received by the key decision-making group is of utmost importance. The closer the decision-making process is to the actual situations in which the decision has to be implemented, furthermore, the higher quality the decision tends to be. Decisions should be made by individuals who are in the midst of the day-to-day action of implementing them. They are the individuals who have the direct experience to know what will and will not work and what should and should not be done. Involvement in decision making also tends to increase staff members' allegiance to the school.

The fifth reason is to increase the commitment of staff members to implement the decision. The effectiveness of the decision depends upon both the logical soundness of the decision and the level of psychological commitment to the decision by the members who have to implement it. Individuals uninvolved in the decision-making group may withhold information the group needs in order to arrive at a high-quality decision, and may put forth only a minimum effort to implement it. A logically sound decision staff members are not committed to implementing is by definition ineffective.

The sixth reason for using cooperative procedures is to change the behavioral patterns and attitudes of staff members. Many of the decisions faced by the school staff are such that changes in their behavioral patterns and attitudes are required to implement the decisions effectively. If you wish to change staff members' behaviors and attitudes, you should involve them in group discussions that lead them to (1) publicly commit themselves to adopt the new attitudes and behave in the new ways and (2) perceive that all other staff members support the new behaviors and attitudes (Johnson & F. Johnson, 1987). How decisions are made will influence how readily faculty will in fact change to implement the decision. Participating in a decision-making discussion within a group can have an impact on a person's subsequent behavior and attitudes.

For these and other reasons, leaders will wish to structure faculty meetings to involve all staff members in the making of the more important decisions.

Ad Hoc Decision-Making Groups

The third type of cooperative group that principals need to use are ad hoc decision-making groups. During faculty meetings the school staff will be asked to make decisions about school policy and what recommendations should be adopted to solve schoolwide problems. The most effective way of making such decisions is to implement a small-group / large-group procedure where staff members first meet in small groups, discuss the issue, and try to reach a decision, and then repeat the process in the staff as a whole. **Ad hoc decision-making groups** are groups temporarily formed to consider an issue and decide by consensus on a recommendation to make to the staff as a whole. More specifically, ad hoc decision-making groups are groups (usually triads) in which staff members:

1. Listen to recommendations made by a schoolwide task force, a school governing council, or an administrator.

2. Decide whether to accept or modify the recommendation and why.

3. Report to the entire faculty their decision and its rationale and listen to the reports of the other triads.

4. Discuss the recommendation in the faculty as a whole and decide (by consensus or majority rule) whether to accept or modify it.

Involving all staff members in the school's decision making through ad hoc decision-making groups ensures that a considered and thoughtful decision is made that everyone is committed to implementing. Making a considered and thoughtful decision is much harder than it sounds. Many times decisions are made by trying to:

1. **Stay with the status quo.** The decision-makers complacently decide to continue whatever they have been doing, clinging to tradition, ignoring information about its ineffectiveness.

2. **Change as little as possible.** The decision-makers adopt a new course of action that requires as little effort to implement as possible.

3. **Delay and avoid making the decision.** The decision-makers believe that they are "damned if they change and damed if they don't." Because they believe there are serious risks no matter what they do, they defensively avoid the decision by (1) procrastination (turning attention away from the conflict to other less-distressing matters), (b) shifting of responsibility or "buck-passing" to someone else (enabling them to evade the dilemma and providing them

with a handy scapegoat should the decision prove to have undesirable outcomes), or (c) psychological escape by means of inventing fanciful rationalizations in support of one of the choice alternatives (selectively attending to only the good aspects of that alternative and ignoring or distorting negative information about it so that decision-makers feel invulnerable to threat and danger). This latter procedure is often known as groupthink.

4. **Choose the first likely solution without considering all alternatives.** The decision-makers feel pressure to make the decision immediately. Fear and anxiety about the consequences of the decision may result in vacillation, panic, and impulsively seizing a hastily contrived solution without understanding its full implications.

These are so easy but so inadequate compared to considered and thoughtful decision making. Considered and thoughtful decision-making can be best achieved from the small-group / large-group decision-making procedure.

The Leader's Role

Organizing the staff into small decision-making groups involves:

1. Specifying the two objectives of (a) making the best decision possible in response to a recommendation made by a schoolwide task force, governing council, or administrator, and (b) improving the ability of faculty to work together to make joint decisions.

2. Making a number of decisions about the staff decision-making groups before the recommendation is considered such as the size of the ad hoc decision-making groups and

the materials each group will need in order to consider thoughtfully the decision.

3. Explaining (a) the decision to be made either adopting or rejecting the recommendation, (b) the positive interdependence of the group, and (c) the ways in which each individual member is accountable to do his or her share of the work.

4. Monitoring the effectiveness of decision-making groups and intervening to provide task assistance (such as answering questions) or to increase staff members' interpersonal and group skills.

5. Having each group report its position and rationale on the recommendation and having groups process how well they worked together.

6. Making the decision in the staff as a whole using consensus, two-thirds vote, or majority vote, depending on which method is most appropriate for the staff.

Objectives

The two objectives of a decision-making group are to make as effective a decision as possible while maintaining good working relationships among staff members. The decision making begins when the task force presents their recommendations to the entire staff. The **purpose of decision making** is to decide on well-considered, well-understood, realistic action toward goals every member wishes to achieve. A **decision** implies that some agreement prevails among group members as to which of several courses of action is most desirable for achieving the group's goals. As stated in the previous chapter, there are five major characteristics of an **effective decision**:

1. The resources of staff members are fully utilized.

2. Time is well used.

3. The decision is correct or of high quality. A **high quality decision** solves the problem, can be implemented in a way that the problem does not reoccur, and does not require more time, people, and material resources than the school can provide.

4. All the required staff members are fully committed to implementing the decision.

5. The problem-solving ability of the staff is enhanced, or at least not lessened.

A decision is effective to the extent that these five criteria are met; if all five are not met, the decision has not been made effectively. More simply, staff members are to make the best decision possible in a way that maximizes their commitment to implement the decision.

Decisions

Deciding On the Size Of The Group. Decision-making groups tend to range in size from two to four. Three is the most frequently used group size. Decision-making groups need to be small enough so that every staff member has to participate actively.

Assigning Staff Members To Groups. Random assignment of staff members to decision-making groups is preferable. The more heterogeneous the decision-making groups, the better, as differences in perspectives will be discussed and talked through in small groups before the whole staff discussion.

Arranging The Room. Members of a decision-making group should sit close enough to each other that they can share materials and talk to each other quietly and maintain eye contact with all group members. Circles are usually best. The principal or leader should have clear access lanes to every group.

Planning Materials. Often task forces will prepare materials to summarize their recommendations and the rationale underlying them. Whatever materials staff members require to consider the recommendation need to be distributed. Materials may be distributed in ways to communicate that the contributions of all group members are required and that staff members are in a "sink or swim together" situation.

Assigning Roles. Cooperative interdependence may also be arranged through the assignment of complementary and interconnected roles to group members. Such roles include a **summarizer** (who restates the group's major conclusions or answers), a **checker** (who ensures that all members can explain how to arrive at an answer or conclusion), and **encourager** (who ensures that all members participate actively in the discussion).

Explaining The Recommendation And The Cooperative Goal Structure

Explaining The Decision-Making Task. The task force members must clearly explain their recommendation. The leader then describes the decision to be made. Staff members must be clear about the decision to be made. The staff is to make a decision as to whether or not to adopt and commit themselves to the recommendation of the task force. The rationale for accepting or rejecting the recommendation must be clearly stated.

Structuring Positive Goal Interdependence. The leader communicates to staff members that they are to have a group goal and must work collaboratively. There is to be one decision from each group, all members must be in agreement, and all members must be able to explain the rationale underlying their decision. Each group will make a presentation of the decision and its rationale to the staff as a whole.

Structuring Individual Accountability. The purposes of the decision-making groups are to make the best decision possible, to understand the rationale for the decision, and to maximize the commitment of each staff member to implementing the decision. To ensure that these purposes are accomplished, each staff member must feel personally responsible for contributing to the quality of the decision and for implementing it to the best of his or her ability. Randomly asking one member of each group to explain to the whole staff their decision and its rationale is one way of doing so.

Specifying Desired Behaviors. Many teachers are not skilled in working effectively with others. Specifying that all group members need to stay with their group, focus on the decision to be made, encourage everyone to participate, paraphrase each other's contributions, summarize, ensure that all members are in agreement and can explain the rationale behind the group's decision, may help teachers to interact effectively.

Monitoring And Intervening

Monitoring Members' Behavior. The leader's job begins in earnest when the decision-making groups begin working. Much of the leader's time is spent observing group members to see what problems they are having reaching consensus and working cooperatively.

Providing Decision-Making Assistance. In monitoring the decision-making groups as they work, leaders will wish to clarify procedures and review important aspects of the recommendation.

Intervening To Teach Cooperative Skills. While monitoring the decision-making groups, leaders often find teachers who do not have the necessary cooperative skills and groups where staff members are having problems in collaborating. In these cases, the leader should intervene to suggest more effective procedures for working together and more effective behaviors in which staff members should engage.

Making And Implementing The Decision

Reporting Decision And Rationale. Each ad hoc group reports its decision and its rationale in the staff meeting.

Making Decision In The Staff As A Whole. After all small groups have reported their decision and its rationale, a general discussion among the entire staff is held and then a decision is made as to whether to accept or modify the task force's recommendations. The decision ideally would be made by consensus, but if time does not allow, the decision may be made by a 2/3 or a simple majority vote.

Providing Closure To The Decision Making. At the end of each faculty meeting, the leader may wish to summarize the major points in the decision and take responsibility for distributing it in writing later.

Implementing The Decision. After the decision is made, it must be implemented. The degree to which staff members implement the decision should be monitored and evaluated by members of the task force.

Group Processing

Assessing How Well The Groups Functioned. The ad hoc decision-making groups should assess how well they worked together and plan how to improve their effectiveness in the future. Our two favorite questions for doing so are: *"What actions helped the group work productively? What actions could be added to make the group even more productive tomorrow?"* A common error of many leaders is to provide too brief a time for staff members to process the quality of their collaboration.

Teaching Staff Members Collaborative Skills

Interpersonal and small group skills are the engine that powers cooperative efforts. For cooperative decision-making groups to be productive, staff members must be able to engage in the needed cooperative skills. Staff members who have never been taught how to work effectively with others cannot be expected to do so. Thus, the first experience of many leaders who structure cooperative decision making is that their teachers cannot collaborate with each other. Yet it is within cooperative situations, where there is a task to complete, that social skills become most relevant and should ideally be taught. All staff members need to become skillful in communicating, building and maintaining trust, providing leadership, and managing conflicts. The interpersonal and small group skills staff members need to master in order to work cooperatively with peers are detailed elsewhere in **Reaching Out: Interpersonal Effectiveness and Self-Actualization**, (Johnson, 1986), **Human Relations And Your Career**, (Johnson, 1987), and **Joining Together: Group Theory and Group Skills** (Johnson & F. Johnson, 1987).

Staff members may be trained in the interpersonal and small group skills necessary for being effective group members in a direct or an indirect way. The **direct** way is to have inservice training programs to teach cooperative skills to staff members. The **indirect** way is to encourage and support the teachers' use of cooperative learning groups in their classes. An important aspect of using cooperative learning groups is training students in the social skills required to "work together to get the job done." By training their students in the social skills needed to learn cooperatively, teachers master the social skills needed to be a supportive colleague.

Summary

Teachers typically are not involved in school decision making. Involving staff members in the decision making of the schools, however, provides the key to:

1. Modelling the use of cooperative procedures.

2. Empowering staff members to face, confront, and solve problems that are too complex for any one staff member to solve alone.

3. Modernizing the school as an organization.

4. Improving the quality of the decisions being made within the school.

5. Increasing the commitment of staff members to implement the decision.

6. Changing the behavioral and attitude patterns of staff members.

For these and other reasons, leaders will wish to structure ad hoc cooperative decision-making groups during faculty meetings to involve all staff members in the making of the more important decisions.

Ad hoc decision-making groups are groups temporarily formed to consider an issue and decide by consensus on a recommendation to make to the staff as a whole. Staff members:

1. Listen to recommendations made by a schoolwide task force, school governing council, or administrator.

2. Decide whether to accept or modify the recommendation and why.

3. Report to the entire faculty their decision and its rationale and listen to the reports of the other triads.

4. Discuss the recommendation in the faculty as a whole and decide whether to accept or modify it.

Organizing the staff into small decision-making groups involves specifying the objectives, making a number of decisions as to the size of groups and the materials they will need to make the decision, explain the task and the positive interdependence to the groups, monitor the effectiveness of the groups in considering the recommendation. The five basic elements of a cooperative group need to be successfully implemented within each ad hoc decision-making group. After the groups are finished, the leader elicits the decision of each triad, and leads the staff into making the decision. For staff members to be effective members of such decision-making groups, they need to learn a variety of interpersonal and small group skills.

Besides empowering staff members through cooperative teams, leaders must lead by example and encourage the heart of staff members to persist in their quest to become better and better teachers. Finally, leaders must keep the dream of the cooperative school alive while simultaneously setting immediate and short-term goals that are attainable.

E
F
F
E
C
T
I
V
E

D
E
C
I
S
I
O
N
-
M
A
K
I
N
G

G
R
O
U
P
S

Decisions

Size of Group
Assigment to Group
Arrangement of Room
Planning of Materials
Assignment of Roles

Explaining the Recommendation and Cooperative Goal Structure

Explaining Decision-Making Task
Structuring Positive Goal Interdependence
Structuring Individual Accountability
Sepcifying Desired Behaviors

Monitoring and Intervening

Monitoring Member's Behavior
Providing Decision-Making Assistance
Intervening to Teach Skills

Making and Implementing Decision

Reporting Decision and Rationale
Making Whole-Staff Decision
Providing Closure
Implementing Decision

Group Processing

Assessing How Well Groups Functioned

Chapter 9

Leading By Example / Encouraging The Heart

Introduction

After challenging the competitive / individualistic status quo, inspiring a mutual vision of the cooperative school, empowering staff members and students through cooperative teamwork, the next steps are to lead by example and encourage the heart of staff members to persist in increasing their expertise in using cooperative learning year after year.

Leading By Example

> *Not the cry, but the flight of the wild duck, leads the flock to fly and follow.*

Chinese Proverb

A skeptic, in the first century of the common era, approached the great rabbi Hillel and asked to be taught the full meaning of the Torah in a single proposition. Hillel responded, **"Do not do onto**

your fellow man what you would not have him do unto you.
This is the essence; the rest is commentary." The same may be
said to leaders. "Do not do onto teachers what you would not have
teachers do unto students. This is the essence; the rest is commentary."

**You can lead others only to where you yourself are willing
to go.** If leaders ask teachers to use cooperative learning, then
leaders must use cooperative procedures. Leaders need to live by
the same rules they propose for staff members. Leaders model the
way. By the clarity of their convictions and by their everyday actions, leaders demonstrate to others how the vision of the cooperative school can be realized.

In other words, leadership is **not** a spectator sport. Leaders do
not sit in the stands and watch. Leaders demonstrate what is important by how they spend their time, by the priorities on their agenda, by the questions they ask, and by the behaviors and results that
they recognize and reward.

Leading by example is done by:

1. **Being clear and enthusiastic about the value of working
   together to get the job done within the classroom and
   within the school.**

2. **Practicing what you preach.** Your words and your actions
   must be consistent.

3. **Presenting a clear plan for how the cooperative school
   will be created.** While the vision is the final destination,
   there must be milestones and signposts that give direction
   to immediate and short-term efforts.

Backing Your Words With Actions

You, the leader, make the vision of the cooperative school tangible by (a) using cooperative procedures and (b) taking risks to increase your professional expertise in structuring cooperative enterprises. Through your consistent promotion and structuring of colleagial support groups, schoolwide task forces, and ad hoc decision-making groups, you model the use of cooperative procedures. Taking risks to increase your expertise in using cooperative teams clearly communicates that you value professional growth.

To model the use of cooperative teams, you must believe in cooperative efforts and personally organize cooperative efforts frequently. **First**, you must be clear about your belief in working together to get the job done and be able to speak coherently about your vision and values. **The more personally enthusiastic you are about cooperative learning the better.** Staff members must know what they are observing and that you consider it important. **Second**, your actions must be congruent with your words. **Your use of cooperative teams demonstrates your commitment to implementing cooperation.** You show your priorities through living your values.

Every exceptional leader we know is a learner. The self-confidence required to lead comes from trying, failing, learning from mistakes, and trying again. Leaders lead by example by being involved in a continuous process of increasing their ability to structure cooperative enterprises. **From making their own journey to actualize the vision of the cooperative school leaders model the way for other staff members.**

The Plan 1: Change Through Incremental Steps

> *"Habits can't be thrown out the upstairs window. They have to be coaxed down the stairs one step at a time."*

> Mark Twain

In addition to the long-term vision of the cooperative school, leaders must have immediate and short-term goals that staff members involved in implementing cooperative learning can obtain. Teachers who wish to use cooperative learning should be encouraged to start small. They should implement cooperative learning in one class, subject area, or unit. Their success should be celebrated and then they should expand to use cooperative learning in another class, subject area, or unit. Small steps that are taken one at a time will result in someday the teacher using cooperative learning the majority of the school day.

When asked how he did it, Don Bennett (the Seattle businessperson who climbed to the top of Mount Rainier on one leg) replied (Kouzes & Posner, 1987): *"One hop at a time. I imagined myself on top of that mountain one thousand times a day in my mind. But when I started to climb it, I just said to myself, 'Anyone can hop from here to there.' And I would. And when the going got roughest, and I was really exhausted, that's when I would look down at the path ahead and say to myself, 'You just have to take one more step, and anybody can do that.' And I would."*

Long journeys are accomplished one step at a time. With each small step the person feels a little more successful in achieving the goal and a little more committed to continuing the effort. **At the heart of change are two themes: small successes and incremental commitment.**

Using cooperative learning needs to be broken down into small, doable steps that allow teachers to say **yes** numerous times, not just once. Leaders understand how critical it is to break the implementation process down into small steps so that they are easily understood and completed. If implementing cooperative learning is conceived too broadly, teachers will be overwhelmed. Getting teachers to change from an individualistic / competitive teaching pattern to cooperative learning proceeds step by step. The most effective change processes are incremental. Staff members need to identify the place they will get started. Starting must be doable within their existing skill and resource levels. Once they have taken the starting step they must feel successful. **Small successes** are concrete, complete, implemented actions toward using cooperative learning. Teachers plan a cooperative lesson, celebrate their success in doing so, teach the lesson, and celebrate their success in doing so. One hop at a time is all it takes.

The success of behavior-change programs such as Alcoholics Anonymous and Weight Watchers is due in large part to their incremental change philosophies. Participants are not told to become totally abstinent for the rest of their lives. Although this is their goal, members are told to stay sober one day at a time or one hour at a time if temptation is severe. The seemingly impossibility of lifetime abstinence is scaled down to the more workable task of not taking a drink for twenty-four hours. This drastically reduces the size of the success necessary to stay sober.

Incremental commitment is the increased determination to use cooperative learning resulting from small successes. Getting staff members to take action is at the heart of the commitment process. To act is to commit onself. Leaders get and keep staff members committed to implementing cooperative learning. **First**, staff members should be given a choice to use cooperative learning or not. If they volunteer to implement cooperative learning, it must be their own choice. They should not feel forced to do so. Free choice involves having the alternative of not using cooperative learning, understanding that it will require effort on their part to attain expertise in using cooperative learning, and volunteering to do so.

Second, the choice should be visible to colleagues. Becoming part of a colleagial support group makes a staff member's implementation efforts visible and observable. Testimonials in Weight Watchers, for example, makes a person's level of commitment quite visible to others. Visibility makes it nearly impossible for staff members to deny their choice or to claim that they forgot about it. Leaders ensure that staff members "go public" with their implementation of cooperative learning.

Third, the choice to implement cooperative learning must be a choice that cannot be easily changed. Choices that are hard to change increase staff members' investment in the decision. Such choices are not trivial. Thus, volunteering to implement cooperative learning should entail membership in a colleagial support group that meets weekly (or more frequently) and participation in an ongoing training program that is hard to drop out of. Taking actions that cannot be retrieved requires staff members to find and accept salient arguments that support and justify it, creating a strong internalized rationale that deepens personal responsibility and belief in the correctness of implementing cooperative learning. Getting involved in helping a colleague implement cooperative learning, in addition, makes it more difficult to stop using cooperative learning. Publicizing the implementation efforts of staff members further increases the difficulty of using cooperative learning less and less frequently.

Fourth, staff members need to feel successful in their implementation efforts. Every lesson they plan and conduct should increase their confidence in their ability to use cooperative learning effectively and should be celebrated by their colleagial support group and leader. Small successes accumulate into large, sustained efforts Be certain to make their progress very visible.

Finally, reduce the cost of volunteering. Implementing cooperative learning requires staff members to take risks. Mistakes will be made. It is easier for staff members to say "yes" when leaders can minimize the costs of their potential mistakes. In teaching would-be pilots to fly an airplane, for example, a friend of ours lets them make mistakes, but she doesn't let them crash. **Most educators are "risk aversive," so it is more important to reduce the negative consequences of new actions than to enhance the positive consequences.** Reducing the costs of failure makes it easier to take the first step.

The Plan 2: Making Cooperative Learning Doable

The initial steps in implementing cooperative learning should be doable. This requires training in how to structure and conduct cooperative learning lessons. There is nothing more discouraging than being confronted initially with tasks that teachers do not know how to do and at which they know they will fail. **In order for teachers to gain full expertise in using cooperative learning, both long-term training over a number of years and an active colleagial support group enhancing teacher's use of**

tive learning are needed. Leaders need to have a long-term time perspective on the professional growth of staff members. At least a three-year training program needs to be conducted.

The **first year training program** should follow a general pattern. An awareness session is conducted to inform most staff members of the nature of cooperative learning. "Scouts" are then recruited in teams to form a colleagial support group and participate in the basic training of at least 40 hours (5 days) (Johnson, Johnson, & Holubec, 1988a). The basic training includes the basic definitions and procedures for using cooperative learning, a description of the teacher's role, the research evidence providing a rationale for using cooperative learning, how to ensure students believe it is "sink or swim together," how to teach students social skills, the ways in which groups process how well they are working, and the importance of establishing a colleagial support group. On the basis of this training teachers feel able to begin using cooperative learning procedures and to teach students the social and cognitive skills they need to work effectively with each other. Each teacher is encouraged to be part of a colleagial support group that meets regularly to improve each member's expertise in using cooperative learning groups.

From the training program teachers are empowered by an increased understanding of what cooperative learning is and how it may be implemented and from the colleagial support group teachers are empowered by commitment--the passion, motivation, and vision necessary to persevere responsibly in the face of discouragement and difficulty.

Volunteering to be trained in cooperative learning procedures and then to use cooperative learning in a lesson is to commit oneself. Getting teachers to take action is the heart of the commitment process. Leaders induce and maintain teachers' commitment to using cooperative learning. Being part of a training program induces commitment to implement cooperative learning by reflecting a public choice to implement cooperative learning, that is visible to colleagues and cannot be reversed very easily.

The **second year**, the "scouts" should receive at least 40 more hours of training that includes advanced uses of cooperative learning procedures (e.g., as part of lecturing and direct teaching and as permanent base groups that allow for ongoing caring and committed relationships), the integrated use of cooperative, competitive, and individualistic learning activities within the same instructional unit; the teaching of advanced social skills such as leadership, trust-building, and communication; and the solution of problems involved in implementing cooperative learn ing (Johnson, Johnson, & Holubec, 1988b). The purposes of this training are to continue the teachers' use of cooperative learning procedures and enable them to build a coherent instructional system that includes different types of cooperative learning groups and an integration of cooperative, competitive, and individualistic learning. In addition, it increases the teachers' skills in instructing students in the social and cognitive skills they need to work effectively within cooperative learning groups.

In addition to the "scouts," a second set of volunteers participate in the basic training. Simultaneously, they are "networked" with the "scouts" in their building and included in the ongoing colleagial support groups.

The **third year**, teachers should receive 40 hours of additional training on how to (1) structure academic / intellectual conflicts to increase students' motivation to learn and ability to think critically, and (2) train students in negotiation and mediation procedures and skills in order to establish a peer mediation program (Johnson & Johnson, 1987a).

A third set of volunteers participate in the basic training. Simultaneously, they are "networked" with the experienced teachers in their building and included in the ongoing colleagial support groups.

While teachers are implementing cooperative learning their successes in doing so need to be recognized and celebrated. When small successes are recognized and appreciated, a heightened interest in continuing with the journey is built.

Encouraging The Heart

The word **encouragement** has its root in the Latin word **cor**, meaning "heart." When leaders encourage staff members, through recognition and celebration, they inspire them with courage--with heart.

Implementing cooperative learning is hard work. Improving one's use of cooperative learning and other teaching strategies year after year is hard work. Leaders inspire staff members to have the hope and courage to continue the quest. Their tools are individual recognition for working to achieve the vision, individual pride, group celebrations, and love.

It is not unusual for highly committed individuals to report working sixty-, seventy-, and even eighty-hour work weeks. Along the way, they are tempted to give up. To persist in increasing expertise in cooperative learning, teachers need encouragement. They need the heart to continue with the journey.

There are five steps in encouraging the heart:

1. Recognize the individual contributions to the common vision.

2. Have frequent group celebrations of individual and joint accomplishments.

3. Be a cheerleader for teachers implementing cooperative learning.

4. Create social support systems that give members the courage to change their teaching practices and increase their expertise in using cooperative learning groups and celebrate their successes in doing so.

5. Love seeing students and staff members working together to get the job done and love the people working hard to achieve the vision of the cooperative school.

Leadership By Walking Around

Outstanding companies get the executives out of the office and into the workplace. Executives are encouraged to "walk around" and observe workers in action. If the business of the schools occurs in the classroom, where should we find the leader?

When leaders pops into classrooms for a quick visit they have three purposes. The first is to increase teachers' sense of self-efficacy by increasing their belief that they can implement cooperative learning successfully. The second is to increase their commitment for doing so. The third is to build trust with the teacher being observed. Each visit should build an expectation of a positive experience the next time the leader "pops in." Negative feedback decreases self-efficacy, commitment, and trust. Feedback, therefore, has to be positive. If there is time, furthermore, the leader wants to ask the teacher questions about the lesson that causes the teacher to think meta-cognitively about it.

There is a tremendous power in regular, positive peer recognition. The cooperative school is designed to produce lots of success in using cooperative learning and recognition when it occurs. Extraordinary use of interpersonal incentives are used. With hoopla whenever possible.

An important way that leaders give heart to others is by recognizing individual contributions to the common vision. What makes a difference to each individual staff member is to know that his or her successes are perceived, recognized, and celebrated. Leaders search out "good news" opportunities. Implementing cooperative learning is an arduous and long-term enterprise. Teachers become exhausted, frustrated, and disenchanted. They often are tempted to give up. Leaders must inspire teachers to continue the journey by encouraging their hearts. It is the leader's responsibility to show staff members that they can succeed in implementing cooperative learning. Leaders must catch staff members doing things right and recognize them.

Leaders need to be in and out of classrooms observing teachers frequently in order to provide immediate and relevant praise and compliments. Recognition is most effective when it is specific and in close proximity to the appropriate behavior. In order to provide timely and specific feedback and recognition you have to go out and find teachers conducting cooperatively structured lesson. Being out and about allows you personally to observe teachers conducting cooperative lessons and recognizing their efforts on the spot.

Visits to classrooms do not have to be long. Leaders can walk through, spending a few minutes observing, recognizing something good about the cooperative lesson, and moving on to another classroom. A note highlighting something positive about the lesson may be left in the teacher's box as a form of feedback. And recognition may be expressed. Carol Cummings (1985) reports one high school principal gave coupons for 15 minutes of released time (a teacher could leave school early or arrive late) for something good observed during a walk-through.

If you do not show your appreciation to staff members, they are going to stop caring, and then, in essence, you are going to find yourself out of business.

Group Celebrations

The second step in encouraging the heart is to have many celebrations, both spontaneous and scheduled. While many celebrations are, and should be, spontaneous, some celebrations should be scheduled. Cooperative Learning Day may be an annual event, scheduled on the same day each year and put on the school calendar. Putting a discussion of cooperative learning on the faculty meeting, PTA, and school board agendas is another way to celebrate the success teachers are having implementing cooperative learning. Newsletters to parents can include articles on the success the school is having in using cooperative learning. Informal discussions with staff members can include praise for a cooperative learning lesson observed. Leaders give visible and public praise for teachers using cooperative learning. They are enthusiastic about it. Remember, **you can't light a fire with a wet match**.

Leaders should be masters of celebration. They should give out stickers, t-shirts, buttons, and every other conceivable award when staff members achieve a milestone in implementing cooperative learning. Leaders find ways to celebrate accomplishments, preferably with hoopla. Most important of all, interpersonal recognition is emphasized. There is nothing more motivating than having colleagues cheering you on and jointly celebrating your successes. In excellent schools, such positive confirmation is used extensively.

Group celebrations require a cooperative structure such as a colleagial support group. In competitions, to declare one staff member a success is to declare other staff members losers. Celebrations will only work in giving staff members the heart to persist in implementing cooperative learning within cooperative teams.

Celebrations create positive interaction among school staff, providing concrete evidence that people care about each other. Within cooperative enterprises, it is genuine acts of caring that draw people together and forward. Love of teaching, students, and each other is what inspires many staff members to commit more and more of their energy to their jobs. Knowing that you are not alone in your efforts and that you can count on others if necessary provides the courage to continue in times of turmoil and stress.

Cheerleading

The third step in encouraging the heart is leading the cheering for the teachers implementing cooperative learning. Cheerleading involves more than shouting "hurrahs." To cheerlead you must be clear about valuing cooperative learning and what the difference is between well-structured and poorly structured cooperative lessons. You have to be able to recognize the five basic elements of a good cooperative lesson. And it helps to have some symbolic rewards for good efforts, such as t-shirts, flowers, plaques, certificates, pats-on-the-back, notes of recognition, and so forth. When other people cheerlead, join in the fun and be a part of it. Let others know that it is okay to laugh, have fun, and enjoy each other's company.

Cheerleading is a large part of the leader's function. Encouraging the heart is not only the process of recognizing individual achievements. It also includes celebrating the efforts of the colleagial support groups. Cheerleading and celebrating are the processes of honoring people and sharing with them in the sweet taste of success. When leaders cheerlead, they base their celebrations on three central principles: (1) focusing on key values, (2) making recognition publicly visible, and (3) being personally involved.

Determining what you want to celebrate is the starting point for cheerleaders. Leaders cheer about the implementation of cooperative learning in the classroom. Every time a teacher conducts a lesson, replans a unit to revolve around cooperative learning, and helps and supports a colleague to use cooperative learning procedures, leaders should lead the cheering.

Events that are public make a leader's actions more visible to others and, therefore, have a stronger effect. Celebrations and cheerleading are public events. They enhance the commitment to key school values and demonstrate visibly to others that the school is serious about the implementation of cooperative learning. Public ceremonies and rituals are the ingredients that crystallize personal commitment. They help bond staff members together and let them know that they are not alone. There is a family feeling about celebrations. While fun, they also provide a meaningful reminder about which key values are celebrated in the school.

Create Social Support

The fourth step in encouraging the heart is to build social support systems for the staff members implementing cooperative learning and for yourself. Regular meetings of the colleagial support group are the foundation for social support among members. Social interaction increases people's commitments to the standards of the group, and during the meetings consensus about various ways of using cooperative learning and the pressure for every member to do their fair share are developed. And when teachers get discouraged the social support increases their commitment to persist in the hard work required to gain expertise in the use of cooperative learning. Group celebrations help. Every time staff members celebrate each other's success in implementing cooperative learning they increase their own commitment to do so.

There is a myth that leaders should not fraternize with followers. In the military there are officer clubs and clubs for nonofficers. The military perspective frowns on friendships between officers and subordinates. They have a strict "class" system where the upper-class does not associate with the lower-class except to order them around. Such an approach does not work in the schools. **Implementing cooperative learning requires everyone to pitch in and work together.** When colleagial support groups form to implement cooperative learning you, the leader, need to include yourself in. Staff members should see you as their colleague as well as a leader. Working together to get the job done increases the social support among all individuals involved. Be part of the team. Make sure you are not isolated from the rest of the school staff.

In the process of celebrating accomplishments, leaders create social support networks. People who share the same goals are likely to come to care about one another on more than just a professional level. Extraordinary accomplishments are not achieved without everyone--including the leader--getting personally involved with the task and with each other. Genuine personal relationships are formed among members of the team.

Social support serves to enhance not only productivity but also psychological well-being and physical health. Social support not only enhances wellness but also buffers against disease, particularly during times of high stress.

Stay In Love

> *Love is loyalty. Love is teamwork. Love respects the dignity of the individual. Heartpower is the strength of your corporation.*

Vince Lombardi

William Manchester wrote of an insight he had on revisiting Sugar Loaf Hill in Okinawa, where 34 years before he had fought as a Marine. He stated that he understood, at last, why he secretly left a military hospital and, in violation of orders, returned to the front and almost certain death. He stated, *"It was an act of love. Those men on the line were my family, my home. They were closer to me than I can say, closer than any friends had been or ever would be. They were comrades; three of them had saved my life. They had never let me down, and I couldn't do it to them. I had to be with them, rather than let them die and me live with the knowledge that I might have saved them."* He concluded that men do not fight for flag or country, for the Marine Corps or glory or any other abstraction. *"They fight for their friends."*

The fifth step in encouraging the heart is to be in love with implementing cooperative learning to benefit students and implementing cooperative teams to benefit staff members so that their actions will, in turn, benefit students. Ask yourself, **"Are you in this job to do something, or are you in this job for something to do?"** Thomas J. Watson, the founder of IBM, once stated that you have to put your heart in the business and the business in your heart. Many outstanding leaders state, "I love what I'm doing." Ask yourself, "What is it about cooperative learning that I love." "What is it about working together to get the job done that I passionately believe in?"

Leadership is an affair of the heart, not the head. Leaders are in love with their fellow staff members and the students in the school. Leadership is personal. To encourage teachers to use cooperative learning they must believe you care about them personally.

Expectations for committed work are communicated primarily through socioemotional support and encouragement. Treating people in a friendly, encouraging, and positive fashion and being attentive to their needs produces increased understanding of being expected to perform at one's best and increased motivation to do so.

Kouzes and Posner (1987) report a conversation with U. S. Army Major General John H. Stanford. They asked him how he would develop leaders. He replied, *"Whenever anyone asks me that question I tell them I have the secret to success in life. The secret to success is to stay in love. Staying in love gives you the fire to really ignite other people, to see inside other people, to have a greater desire to get things done than other people. A person who is not in love doesn't really feel the kind of excitement that helps them to get ahead and lead others and to achieve. I don't know any other fire, any other thing in life that is more exhilarating and is more positive a feeling than love is."*

Summary

Leading by example is done by:

1. Being clear and enthusiastic about the value of working together to get the job done within the classroom and within the school.

2. Practicing what you preach. Your words and your actions must be consistent. You must use colleagial support

groups, school-wide task forces, and ad hoc decision-making groups frequently and consistently. You must be a leader, taking risks in improving your competence In implementing cooperative teams at the building level.

3. Presenting a clear plan for how the cooperative school will be created. While the vision is the final destination, there must be milestones and signposts that give direction to immediate and short-term efforts. There are two parts to the plan. The first is having staff members implement cooperative learning in small, incremental steps. The second is to make implementing cooperative learning doable by having an ongoing training program and colleagial support groups to provide help and assistance in applying what is learned in the training within participants' classes.

There are five steps in encouraging the heart:

1. Recognize the individual contributions of staff members to the common vision.

2. Have frequent group celebrations of individual and joint accomplishments in implementing cooperative learning.

3. Be a cheerleader for teachers implementing cooperative learning to ensure that their hard work is recognized and respected by their colleagues.

4. Create social support systems that give members the courage to change their teaching practices and increase their expertise in using cooperative learning groups and celebrate their successes in doing so.

5. Love seeing students and staff members working together to get the job done and love the staff members and students working hard to achieve the vision of the cooperative school.

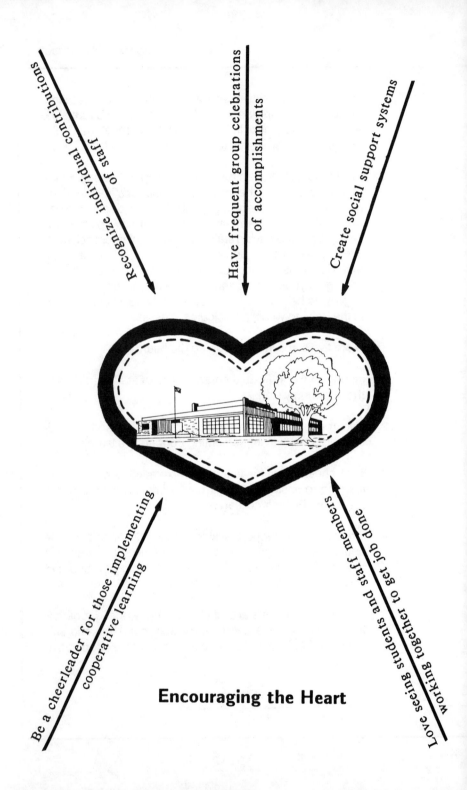

Recognize individual contributions of staff

Have frequent group celebrations of accomplishments

Create social support systems

Be a cheerleader for those implementing cooperative learning

Love seeing students and staff members working together to get job done

Encouraging the Heart

Chapter 10

The Stars And The Ground

Introduction

Aesop tells a tale of an astrologer who believed he could read the future in the stars. One evening he was walking along an open road, his eyes fixed on the stars, when he fell into a pit full of mud and water. Up to his ears in the muddy water, he clawed at the slippery sides of the pit. Unable to climb out he cried for help. As the villagers pulled him out of the mud, one of them said, *"What use is it to read the future in the stars if you can not see the present in the ground at your feet?"*

What Aesop failed to point out in this fable is that you do not have to make an either-or choice. You must be able to simultaneously focus on the future vision of a cooperative school and see each little step required to get there. Leaders look to the stars and to the ground in front of your feet at the same time! They make the vision of the future compelling and exciting. At the same time, they set immediate and short-term goals that are attainable. They create small successes that incrementally increase staff members' commitment to achieving the cooperative school. They move to the vision one hop at a time.

Leading The Cooperative School

Schools are not buildings, curriculums, and machines. **Schools are relationships and interactions among people.** How the interpersonal interaction is structured determines how effective schools are. There are three ways that school relationships may be structured: competitively (so that individuals compete to see who is best), individualistically (everyone works on their own independent from each other), and cooperatively (so that individuals work together to achieve mutual goals). The leader's responsibilities include ensuring that the interpersonal interactions are oriented toward cooperatively achieving the goals of the school.

An essential skill that all leaders need is knowing how to structure situations cooperatively. This takes leadership. **You demonstrate leadership by**:

1. Challenging the status quo of the competitive / individualistic tradition.

2. Inspiring a vision of what the school could be if cooperative learning for students and cooperative teaming for staff members were used frequently and consistently.

3. Empowering teachers by organizing them into cooperative teams (e.g., colleagial support groups, task forces, and ad hoc decision-making groups) and empowering students by organizing them into cooperative learning groups.

4. Leading by example by modeling the use of cooperative procedures.

5. Encouraging staff members to have the heart to continue their quest to be better and better cooperative learning teachers.

The success of such leadership creates the cooperative school. The **cooperative school** consists of cooperative learning within the classroom and cooperative efforts within the staff. **To qualify as a cooperative school, cooperation must dominate both student and faculty life.** This requires quite a transformation. Classrooms are dominated by competitive / individualistic learning. Staffs are dominated by competitive / individualistic relations. Given the loosely-coupled nature of the school, leaders cannot order teachers to teach cooperatively. They can only inspire it. To create a cooperative school, individuals must lead, not manage.

What teachers advocate to students, they will tend to adopt in their interaction with colleagues. When teachers advocate competition and individualistic efforts within their classrooms, they will tend to act competitively and individualistically with peers. Although the competitive / individualistic orientation has dominated American schools for the past 50 years, cooperation is now being rediscovered. The considerable research validating the effectiveness of cooperation has been organized and synthesized. Dozens of new research studies are being conducted each year. Clear procedures for teachers to follow in structuring cooperation among students have been developed, field tested, and perfected. Clear procedures for leaders to follow in structuring cooperation among staff members are now being developed, field tested, and perfected. The myths supporting the overuse and inappropriate use of individualistic and competitive learning are being dispelled.

The intent of this book is to provide a model for leading a cooperative school.

Challenge The Status Quo

Schools have been loosely-coupled organizations in which goals are ambiguous, staff members function independently from each other, are not accountable to each other, and rarely process how effectively the staff is functioning as a unit. This organizational structure is not responsive to changes in the nature of students, the advances in teaching procedures, and the changing nature of the world in which students will have to live. **The organizational nature of the school needs to be transformed into a cooperative one in order to increase productivity, promote more caring and committed relationships, increase social support, and increase professional self-esteem.** The transformation of the school from a place dominated by competitive / individualistic orientations to a cooperative organization increases staff members' commitment to increase their professional competence and expertise.

Create A Shared Vision

The leader is the **keeper of the dream** who inspires commitment to work hard toward actualizing a common vision. In order to be compelling, the vision must be rational, that is, based on a coherent theory that is validated by research. The leader must be able to communicate the fact that more research (over 550 studies) has been conducted on the relative effectiveness of cooperative, competitive, and individualistic efforts than on almost any other aspect of educational practice. We know more about the effectiveness of cooperative learning than we do about age grouping, starting school at age 6, the 50-minute period, departmentalization, lecturing, seat work, home work, or parental involvement. Working together to get the job done results in higher achievement, more frequently higher-level reasoning, more positive attitudes toward the work being done, greater social skills, greater psychological health, higher self-esteem, and better relationships with peers and superiors.

Empower Students Through Cooperative Learning

Students are empowered through cooperative learning groups. Many students feel unable to do high-level work and to understand complex material. Many students feel helpless and discouraged. Giving them cooperative learning partners provides hope, opportunity, and assistance. **The heart of cooperative learning groups is five basic elements: positive interdependence, face-to-face (promotive) interaction, individual accountability, social skills, and group processing.** Formal, informal, and base cooperative learning groups may be used in the classroom. Within formal cooperative learning groups the teacher's role involves making a set of preinstructional decisions such as how large groups will be and how students will be assigned to groups, clearly explaining the cooperative goal structure and the learning task, monitoring students as they work, and evaluating students' performance. Informal cooperative learning groups are used to ensure that students stay intellectually active during lectures. Base groups provide the permanent and long-term relationships that ensure academic progress is made by all students. Building a cooperative school requires that the majority of the classes are dominated by cooperative learning.

Empowering Staff Members Through Cooperative Teams

The heart of school effectiveness is teacher's instructional expertise. The leader's primary responsibility is to work to increase the instructional expertise of staff members. This requires an understanding of procedural learning--teachers must both understand the nature of cooperative learning and be able to implement it within their classes--and the progressive refinement model for gaining expertise. **Teachers progressively refine their expertise in implementing cooperative learning by being willing to take the risk of teaching cooperatively structured lessons, assessing the consequences of teaching lessons cooperatively, reflecting on how to improve implementation of cooperative learning, and teaching a modified lesson.** Teachers should then share what they have learned about implementing cooperative learning with colleagues. Gaining and maintaining expertise is an interpersonal process that requires supportive and encouraging colleagues.

The most important aspect of providing leadership is empowering teachers by organizing them into cooperative teams. Three types of cooperative teams are necessary: colleagial support groups to encourage and support each other's efforts to use cooperative learning, task forces to make recommendations about how to deal with schoolwide issues such as curriculum revision and communication with parents, and ad hoc decision-making groups to involve all staff members in the important school decisions.

Colleagial Support Groups

Increasing professional expertise requires colleagial support groups aimed at increasing members' competence in implementing cooperative learning. The implementation of cooperative learning needs to be coupled with the implementation of colleagial support groups among teachers. Both the success of implementation efforts and the quality of life within most schools depend on teachers and other staff members cooperating with each other. Colleagial relationships take as careful structuring and monitoring as does cooperative learning.

In order for a colleagial support group (or any cooperative team) to function effectively, there must be clear positive interdependence, face-to-face promotion interaction among members, individual accountability, appropriate use of social skills, and the processing of how effective the group is functioning.

Schoolwide Task Forces

For many schoolwide issues such as curriculum revision and communication with parents, task forces need to be organized. Task forces carefully consider and research the issue and make a recommendation to the staff as a whole. To be effective task forces need to collect valid and complete information about the problem, engage in controversy to ensure that all alternative solutions get a fair hearing, synthesize the best points from all perspectives, and make a free and informed choice of which alternative solution to adopt. Members must have continuing motivation to solve the problem so that a new recommendation may be made if the initial plan does not work.

Ad Hoc Decision-Making Groups

Ad hoc decision-making groups then consider the recommendations of the task forces and decide whether to accept or modify the proposed solution. Staff members are assigned to temporary cooperative decision-making triads during a faculty meeting. Each ad-hoc group then reports its decision to the entire faculty, a discussion is held, and then a staff decision is made by consensus.

Leading By Example

To provide school leadership, you need to lead by example. Leading by example requires that you (a) use cooperative procedures through organizing staff members into cooperative teams and (b) take risks to increase professional expertise. You strive to be a role model who exemplifies the organizational and leadership values you believe are important. Your priorities show through what you do. The self-confidence required to lead comes from trying, failing, learning from mistakes, and trying again. From making your own journey to actualize your vision, you model the way for staff members and students.

Encouraging The Heart

Long-term committed efforts come from the heart, not the head. It takes courage and hope to continue the quest. Striving for increased expertise is an arduous and long-term enterprise. Individuals become exhausted, frustrated, and disenchanted. They are tempted to give up.

Leaders are vigilant about the little things that make a big difference. **What makes a difference to each member of the school is to know that his or her successes are perceived, recognized, and celebrated.** Hope and courage are given by recognizing individual contributions to the common vision and frequently having group celebrations of individual and joint accomplishments. Leaders search out "good news" opportunities and orchestrate celebrations of how well cooperative learning is being implemented in classrooms and how well cooperative teaming is being implemented in the school.

Leaders care about their colleagues and encourage colleagues to care about each other and all students. The caring relationships provide the heart to continue improving expertise in implementing cooperative learning year after year after year. Within cooperative enterprises it is genuine acts of caring that draw people together and forward. **Love of teaching, students, and each other is what inspires staff members to commit more and more of their energy to their jobs.** Establishing a cooperative structure and encouraging the development of caring and committed relationships is one of the best-kept secrets of exemplary leadership.

Leaping The Abyss Of Failure

Leaders give teachers the courage they need to take the risks necessary to gain expertise in implementing cooperative learning in their classes and work cooperatively with their colleagues. Teachers can choose to play it safe in the short-run by traveling on the path of the status quo, thereby facing guaranteed long-term failure through trying to educate students with obsolete and outdated competitive and individualistic procedures. **Managers** organize the easy walk downward along the path of the status quo. **Leaders** encourage and inspire teachers to take the difficult leaps toward increased competence.

References

Allen, V. (1976). **Children as teachers: Theory and research on tutoring.** New York: Academic Press.

Ames, G., & Murray, F. (1982). When two wrongs make a right: Promoting cognitive change by social conflict. **Developmental Psychology, 18**, 892-895.

Anderson, L. (1984). What teachers don't do and why. **Education Report** (University of South Carolina), **27** (December), 1, 4.

Annis, L. (1983). The processes and effects of peer tutoring. **Human Learning, 2**, 39-47.

Aronson, E. (1978). The theory of cognitive dissonance: A current perspective. In L. Berkowitz (Ed.), **Cognitive theories in social psychology.** New York: Academic Press.

Aronson, E., Blaney, N., Stephan, C., Sikes, J., & Snapp, M. (1978). **The jigsaw classroom.** Beverly Hills, CA: Sage.

Aronson, E., & O'Leary, M. (1982-83). The relative effectiveness of models and prompts on energy conservation: A field experiment in a shower room. **Journal of Environmental Systems, 12**, 219-224.

Ashton, P., & Webb, R. (1986). **Making a difference: Teachers' sense of efficacy and student achievement.** New York: Longman.

Bargh, J., & Schul, Y. (1980). On the cognitive benefits of teaching. **Journal of Educational Psychology, 72**, 593-604.

Benware, C. (1975). Quantitative and qualitative learning differences as a function of learning in order to teach another. Unpublished manuscript, University of Rochester. (Cited in Deci, E., **Intrinsic motivation.** New York: Plenum Press.

Berman, P., & McLaughlin, M. (1978). **Federal programs supporting educational change, Vol. VIII: Implementing and sustaining innovations.** Santa Monica, CA: Rand Corporation.

Blake, R., & Mouton, J. (1961). Comprehension of points of communality in competing solutions. **Sociometry, 25,** 56-63.

Blake, R., & Mouton, J. (1974). Designing change for educational institutions through the D/D matrix. **Education and Urban Society, 6,** 179-204.

Blumberg, A., May, J., & Perry, R. (1974). An inner-city school that changed--and continued to change. **Education and Urban Society, 6,** 222-238.

Borgida, E., & Nisbett, R. (1977). The differential impact of abstract vs. concrete information decision. **Journal of Applied Social Psychology, 7,** 258-271.

Bronowski, J. (1973). **The ascent of man.** Boston: Little/Brown.

Collins, B. (1970). **Social psychology.** Reading, MA: Addison-Wesley.

Crawford, J., & Haaland, G. (1972). Predecisional information seeking and subsequent conformity in the social influence process. **Journal of Personality and Social Psychology, 23,** 112-119.

Cummings, C. (1985). **Peering in on peers.** Edmonds, WA: Teaching.

Deutsch, M. (1949). A theory of cooperation and competition. **Human Relations, 2,** 129-152.

Deutsch, M. (1962). Cooperation and trust: Some theoretical notes. In M. Jones (Ed.), **Nebraska symposium on motivation** (pp. 275-320). Lincoln, NE: University of Nebraska Press.

Deutsch, M. (1973). **The resolution of conflict.** New Haven: Yale University Press.

DeVries, D., & Edwards, K. (1974). Student teams and learning games: Their effects on cross-race and cross-sex interaction. **Journal of Educational Psychology, 66,** 741-749.

Doyle, W. (1983). Academic work. **Review of Educational Research, 53,** 159-199.

Fisher, R. (1969). An each one teach one approach to music notation. **Grade Teacher, 86,** 120.

Gabbert, B., Johnson, D. W., & Johnson, R. (1986). Cooperative learning, group-to-individual transfer, process gain, and the acquisition of cognitive reasoning strategies. **Journal of Psychology, 120,** 265-278.

Gartner, A., Kohler, M., & Reissman, F. (1971). **Children teach children: Learning by teaching.** New York: Harper & Row.

Goldman, S. (1940). Personal manuscript. These papers are now part of the Smithsonian Collection and are quoted by C. Simons in "Supermarkets: How they grew," **The Smithsonian,** 1980, 112.

Goodlad, J. (1983). **A place called school.** New York: Mc-Graw- Hill.

Halverson, R., & Pallak, M. (1978). Commitment, ego-involvement, and resistance to attack. **Journal of Experimental Social Psychology, 14,** 1-12.

Hamill, R., Wilson, T., & Nisbett, R. (1980). Insensitivity to sample bias: Generalizing from a typical case. **Journal of Personality and Social Psychology, 39,** 578-589.

Harkins, S., & Petty, R. (1982). The effects of task difficulty and task uniqueness on social loafing. **Journal of Personality and Social Psychology, 43,** 1214-1229.

Harkins, S., & Petty, R. (in press). The role of intrinsic motivation in eliminating social loafing. **Journal of Personality and Social Psychology.**

Hill, G. (1982). Group versus individual performance: Are N + 1 heads better than one? **Psychological Bulletin, 91,** 517-539.

Ingham, A., Levinger, G., Graves, J., & Peckham, V. (1974). The Ringelmann effect: Studies of group size and group performance. **Journal of Personality and Social Psychology, 10,** 371-384.

Janis, I., & Mann, L. (1977). **Decision-making: A psychological analysis of conflict, choice and commitment.** New York: Free Press.

Johnson, D. W. (1970). **The social psychology of education.** New York: Holt, Rinehart and Winston.

Johnson, D. W. (1974). Communication and the inducement of cooperative behavior in conflicts: A critical review. **Speech Monographs, 41,** 64-78.

Johnson, D. W. (1979). **Educational psychology.** Englewood Cliffs, NJ: Prentice-Hall.

Johnson, D. W. (1986). **Reaching out: Interpersonal effectiveness and self-actualization.** Englewood Cliffs, NJ: Prentice-Hall.

Johnson, D. W. (1987). **Human relations and your career.** Englewood Cliffs, NJ: Prentice-Hall.

Johnson, D. W., & Johnson, F. (1987). **Joining together: Group theory and group skills** (3rd ed.). Englewood Cliffs, NJ: Prentice-Hall.

Johnson, D. W., & Johnson, R. (1974). Instructional goal structure: Cooperative, competitive, or individualistic? **Review of Educational Research, 44,** 213-240.

Johnson, D. W., & Johnson, R. (1975). **Learning together and alone: Cooperative, competitive, and individualistic learning** (1st ed.). Englewood Cliffs, NJ: Prentice-Hall.

Johnson, D. W., & Johnson, R. (1976). Student perceptions of and preferences for cooperative and competitive learning experiences. **Perceptual and Motor Skills, 42,** 989-990.

Johnson, D. W., & Johnson, R. (1978). Social interdependence within instruction. **Journal of Research and Development in Education, 11,** Special issue.

Johnson, D. W., & Johnson, R. (1979). Conflict in the classroom: Controversy and Learning. **Review of Educational Research, 49,** 51-70.

Johnson, D. W., & Johnson, R. (Eds. and Producers) (1980). **Belonging** (16mm color film and VHS video). Edina, MN: Interaction Book Company.

Johnson, D. W., & Johnson, R. (1981). Effects of cooperative and individualistic learning experiences on interethnic interaction. **Journal of Educational Psychology, 73**, 454-459.

Johnson, D.W., & Johnson, R. (1983a). The socialization and achievement crisis: Are cooperative learning experiences the solution? In L. Bickman (Ed.), **Applied social psychology annual 4** (pp. 119-164). Beverly Hills, CA: Sage Publications.

Johnson, D. W., & Johnson, R. (Eds. and producers) (1983b). **Circles of learning** (16mm film and VHS video). Edina, MN: Interaction Book Company.

Johnson, D. W., & Johnson, R. (1984). **Cooperation in the classroom** (1st ed.). Edina, MN: Interaction Book Company.

Johnson, D. W., & Johnson, R. (1985). The internal dynamics of cooperative learning groups. In R. Slavin, S. Sharan, S. Kagan, R. Lazarowitz, C. Webb, and R. Schmuck (eds.), **Learning to cooperate, cooperating to learn** (pp. 103-124). New York: Plenum.

Johnson, D. W., & Johnson, R. (1987a). **Learning together and alone: Cooperative, competitive, and individualistic learning** (2nd ed.). Englewood Cliffs, NJ: Prentice-Hall.

Johnson, D. W., & Johnson, R. (1987b). **Creative conflict.** Edina, MN: Interaction Book Company.

Johnson, D. W., & Johnson, R. (1987c). Research shows the benefits of adult cooperation. **Educational Leadership, 45**, 27-30.

Johnson, D. W., & Johnson, R. (in press). **Cooperation and competition: Theory and research.** Hillsdale, NJ: Lawrence Erlbaum.

Johnson, D. W., Johnson, R., & Holubec, E. (1986). **Circles of learning: Cooperation in the classroom** (revised ed.). Edina, MN: Interaction Book Company.

Johnson, D. W., Johnson, R., & Holubec, E. (eds.) (1987). **Structuring cooperative learning: Lesson plans for teachers.** Edina, MN: Interaction Book Company.

Johnson, D. W., Johnson, R., & Holubec, E. (1988a). **Cooperation in the classroom** (revised ed.). Edina, MN: Interaction Book Company.

Johnson, D. W., Johnson, R., & Holubec, E. (1988b). **Advanced cooperative learning.** Edina, MN: Interaction Book Company.

Johnson, D. W., Johnson, R., & Maruyama, G. (1983). Interdependence and interpersonal attraction among heterogeneous and homogeneous individuals: A theoretical formulcation and a meta-analysis of the research. **Review of Educational Research, 53,** 5-54.

Johnson, D. W., Johnson, R., & Smith, K. (1986). Academic conflict among students: Controversy and learning. In R. Feldman (ed.), **Social psychological applications to education.** Cambridge, MA: Cambridge University Press.

Johnson, D. W., Johnson, R., Smith, K., & Tjosvold, D. (1989). Pro, con, and sysnthesis: Training managers to engage in constructive controversy. In B. Sheppard, M. Bazerman, & R. Lewicki (Eds.) (1989), **Research in negotiation in organization,** Vol. 2. Greenwich, CT: JAI Press.

Johnson, D. W., Johnson, R., Stanne, M., & Garibaldi, A. (in press). Impact of goal and resource interdependence on problem-solving success on a computer-assisted task. **Journal of Social Psychology.**

Johnson, D. W., & Tjosvold, D. (Eds.) (1983). **Productive conflict management.** New York: Irvington Publishers, Inc.

Johnson, D. W., Maruyama, G., Johnson, R., Nelson, D., & Skon, L. (1981). Effects of cooperative, competitive, and individualistic goal structures on achievement: A meta-analysis. **Psychological Bulletin, 89,** 47-62.

Johnson, D. W., Skon, L., & Johnson, R. (1980). The effects of cooperative, competitive, and individualistic goal structures on student achievement on different types of tasks. **American Educational Research Journal, 17,** 83-93.

Johnson, R. (1976). The relationship between cooperation and inquiry in science classrooms. **Journal of Research in Science Teaching, 13,** 55-63.

Johnson, R., & Johnson, D. W. (1973). Cooperation and competition in the classroom. **Elementary School Journal, 74,** 172-181.

Kerr, N. (1983). The dispensibility of member effort and group motivation losses: Free-rider effects. **Journal of Personality and Social Psychology, 44,** 78-94.

Kerr, N., & Bruun, S. (1981). Ringelmann revisited: Alternative explanations for the social loafing effect. **Personality and Social Psychology Bulletin, 7,** 224-231.

Kerr, N., & Bruun, S. (1983). The dispensibility of member effort and group motivation losses: Free-rider effects. **Journal of Personality and Social Psychology, 44,** 78-94.

Kiesler, C. (1971). **The psychology of commitment: Experiments linking behavior to belief.** New York: Academic Press.

Kouzes, J., & Posner, B. (1987). **The leadership challenge.** San Francisco: Jossey-Bass.

Lamm, H., & Grommsdorff, G. (1973). Group versus individual performance on tasks requiring ideational proficiency (brainstorming): A review. **European Journal of Social Psychology, 3**, 361-388.

Langer, E., & Benevento, A. (1978). Self-induced dependence. **Journal of Personality and Social Psychology, 36**, 886-893.

Larson, C., Dansereau, D., O'Donnell, A., Hythecker, V., Lambiotte, J., & Rocklin, T. (1985). Effects of metacognitive and elaborative activity on cooperative learning and transfer. **Contemporary Educational Psychology, 10**, 342-348.

Latane, B., Williams, K., & Harkins, S. (1975). Many hands make for light work: The causes and consequences of social loafing. **Journal of Personality and Social Psychology, 37**, 822-832.

Latane, B., Williams, K., & Harkins, S. (1979, October). Social loafing. **Psychology Today**, 104-110.

Laughlin, P. (1965). Selection strategies in concept attainment as a function of number of persons and stimulus display. **Journal of Experimental Psychology, 70**, 323-327.

Laughlin, P. (1972). Selection versus reception concept-attainment paradigms for individuals and cooperative pairs. **Journal of Educational Psychology, 63**, 116-122.

Laughlin, P., & Jaccard, J. (1975). Social facilitation and observational learning of individuals and cooperative pairs. **Journal of Personality and Social Psychology, 32,** 873-879.

Laughlin, P., & McGlynn, R. (1967). Cooperative versus competitive concept attainment as a function of sex and stimulus display. **Journal of Personality and Social Psychology, 7,** 398-402.

Laughlin, P., McGlynn, R., Anderson, J., & Jacobsen, E. (1968). Concept attainment by individuals versus cooperative pairs as a function of memory, sex, and concept rule. **Journal of Personality and Social Psychology, 8,** 410-417.

Lawrence, G. (1974). **Patterns of effective inservice education: A state of the art summary of research on materials and procedures for changing teacher behaviors in inservice education.** Tallahassee: Florida State Department of Education.

Lew, M., Mesch, D., Johnson, D. W., & Johnson, R. (1986a). Positive interdependence, academic and collaborative-skills group contingencies and isolated students. **American Educational Research Journal, 23,** 476-488.

Lew, M., Mesch, D., Johnson, D. W., & Johnson, R. (1986b). Components of cooperative learning: Effects of collaborative skills and academic group contingencies on achievement and mainstreaming. **Contemporary Educational Psychology, 11,** 229-239.

Lewin, K. (1943). Forces behind food habits and methods of change. The problem of changing food habits. **(NRC Bulletin No. 108).** Washington, DC: National Research Council; Committee on Food Habits.

Little, J. (1982). Norms of collegiality and experimentation: Workplace conditions of school success. **American Educational Research Journal, 19,** 325-340.

Lortie, D. (1975). **Schoolteacher.** Chicago: University of Chicago Press.

Mayer, A. (1903). Uber Einzel-und Gesamtleistung des Schul kindes. **Archiv fur die Gesamte Psychologie, 1,** 276-416.

McGlynn, R. (1972). Four-person group concept attainment as a function of interaction format. **Journal of Social Psychology, 86,** 89-94.

McKeachie, W., Pintrich, P., Lin, Y., & Smith, D. (1986). **Teaching and learning in the college classroom.** Ann Arbor, MI: National Center for Research to Improve Postsecondary Teaching and Learning, University of Michigan.

McLaughlin, M., & Marsh, D. (1978). Staff development and school change. **Teachers College Record, 80,** 69-94.

Mesch, D., Lew, M., Johnson, D. W., & Johnson, R. (1986). Isolated teenagers, cooperative learning, and the training of social skills. **Journal of Psychology, 120,** 323-334.

Moede, W. (1920). **Experimentelle massenpsychologie.** Leipzig: S. Hirzel.

Murray, R. (1983). Cognitive benefits of teaching on the the teacher. Paper presented at American Educational Research Association Annual Meeting, Montreal, Quebec.

Nel, G., Helmreich, R., & Aronson, E. (1969). Opinion change in the advocate as a function of the persuasibility of his audience: A clarification of the meaning of dissonance. **Journal of Personality and Social Psychology, 12,** 117-124.

Nisbett, R., Borgida, E., Crandall, R., & Reed, H. (1976). Popular induction: Information is not always informative. In J. Carrol & J. Payne (Eds.), **Cognition and social behavior.** Hillsdale, NJ: Lawrence Erlbaum.

Pallak, M., Mueller, M., Dollar, K., & Pallak, J. (1972). The effects of commitment on responsiveness to an extreme consonant communication. **Journal of Personality and Social Psychology, 23,** 429-436.

Pallak, M., Sogin, S., & VanZante, A. (1979). Bad decision: The effect of volunteering, locus of causality, and negative consequences on attitude change. **Journal of Personality and Social Psychology, 30,** 217-227.

Pepitone, E. (1980). **Children in cooperation and competition.** Lexington, MA: Lexington Books.

Peters, T., & Waterman, R. (1982). **Search for excellence.** New York: Harper & Row.

Petty, M., Harkins, S., Williams, K., & Latana, B. (1977). Effects of group size on cognitive effort and evaluation. **Journal of Personality and Social Psychology, 3,** 579-582.

Radke, M., & Caso, E. (1948). Lecture and discussion-decision as methods of influencing food habits. **Journal of the American Dietetic Association, 24,** 23-41.

Radke, M., & Klisurich, D. (1947). Experiments in changing food habits. Reported in K. Lewin, Group decision and social change. In E. Maccoby, T. Newcomb, & E. Hartley, (Eds.). **Readings in social psychology.** New York: Henry Holt and Company.

Rogers, E., & Shoemaker, F. (1977). **Communication of innovations: A cross-cultural approach.** New York: Free Press.

Salomon, G. (1981). **Communication and education: Social and psychological interactions.** Beverly Hills, CA: Sage.

Sarason, S. (1971). **The culture of the school and the problem of change.** Boston: Allyn and Bacon.

Sarbin, T. (1976). Cross-age tutoring and social identity. In V. Allen (Ed.), **Children as teachers: Theory and research on tutoring.** New York: Academic Press.

Sharan, S. (1980). Cooperative learning in small groups. **Review of Educational Research, 50,** 241-271.

Sheingold, K., Hawkins, J., & Char, C. (1984). "I'm the thinkist, you're the typist": The interaction of technology and the social life of classrooms. **Journal of Social Issues, 40,** 49-61.

Shulman, L., & Carey, N. (1984). Psychology and the limitations of individual rationality. **Review of Educational Research, 54,** 501-524.

Skon, L., Johnson, D. W., Johnson, R. (1981). Cooperative peer interaction versus individual competition and individualistic efforts: Effects on the acquisition of cognitive reasoning strategies. **Journal of Educational Psychology, 73,** 83-92.

Salatas, H., & Flavell, J. (1976). Retrieval of recently learned information: Development of strategies and control skills. **Child Development, 47,** 941-948.

Slavin, R. (1980). **Using student team learning** (revised ed.). Baltimore, MD: Center for Social Organization of Schools, Johns Hopkins University.

Slavin, R., Leavey, M., & Madden, N. (1983). Combining cooperative learning and individualized instruction: Effects on student mathematics achievement, attitudes, and behaviors. **Elementary School Journal, 84,** 409-422.

Slavin, R. (1983). **Cooperative learning.** New York: Longman.

Spurlin, J., Dansereau, D., Larson, C., & Brooks, L. (1984). Cooperative learning strategies in processing descriptive text: Effects of role and activity level of the learner. **Cognition and Instruction, 1,** 451-463.

Sullivan, J., & Pallak, M. (1976). The effect of commitment and reactance on action-taking. **Personality and Social Psychology Bulletin, 2,** 179-182.

Sweeney, J. (1973). An experimental investigation of the free-rider problem. **Social Science Research, 2,** 277-292.

Thomas, E. (1957). Effects of facilitative role interdependence on group functioning. **Human Relations, 10,** 347-366.

Triplett, N. (1897). The dynamogenic factors in pacemaking and competition. **American Journal of Psychology, 9,** 507-533.

Watson, G., & Johnson, D. W. (1972). **Social psychology: Issues and insights** (2nd ed.). Philadelphia: Lippincott.

Webb, N., Ender, P., & Lewis, S. (1986). Problem-solving strategies and group processes in small group learning computer programming. **American Educational Research Journal, 23,** 245-261.

Wicklund, R., & Brehm, J. (1976). **Perspective on cognitive dissonance.** Hillsdale, NJ: Lawrence Erlbaum.

Willerman, B. (1943). **Group decision and request as means of changing food habits.** A preliminary study directed by Kurt Lewin, Child Welfare Research Station, State University of Iowa, Iowa City.